STEP into
your VISION 2.0

24 Inspirational Leaders Share Their Goal Setting Secrets

Shamayah Sarrucco and Coauthors

Step Into Your Vision 2.0
24 Inspirational Leaders Share Their Goal Setting Secrets

Copyright © 2014 by Shamayah Sarrucco

Published by
Komera Press
200 104th Avenue, Suite 143
Treasure Island, Florida 33706
KomeraPress.com
Orders@KomeraPress.com

If you are serious about achieving your goals, download your FREE GIFT that can change your life at www.HappinessisaVerb.com/SIYV2.0

ACKNOWLEDGEMENTS

With joy in my heart, I want to express my deepest gratitude…

To you, our reader, for picking this book up and reading these words. *Thank you for your trust and your willingness to be inspired to make your life and business even better!*

To the amazing people who have contributed to the realization of this book and are traveling with me on this exciting journey called life:

My dear mom, who has cultivated in me the love for books, the desire to learn, and the determination never to give up on my dreams. *Thank you, Mom, for your love and support.*

The most fabulous, fun, and smartest sisters in the whole world—Tanya, Elmy, Terya, and Sharryl. *Thank you for love and friendship.*

My extraordinary mentor and dear friend, Meir Ezra, for teaching me the profound yet simple tools to *truly* step into my vision and create an incredible life. *Thank you Meir for seeing my ability and directing me on my path!*

The incredible team who made this such a great book. *Thank you so much!*

My precious friends Ken Daniel, Dan Vega, Aneissa van Metre, Cathy Slaght, Donovan Thompson, Ralph Pawl, Jeff Cesal and Diana Garrett. *Thank you for being there for me. You'll always have a special place in my heart.*

Last, but not least, each one of the great authors who were willing to share their story and lessons with the world. *Thank you! This book would not be the same without you!*

TABLE OF CONTENTS

Introduction

"We can make a living or design a life." – Jim Rohn

*W*hat beautiful desires do you have in your heart? Is there someone you love that you would like to provide for? Or maybe you want to pay for your children's college education? Are there far away countries on your bucket list you want to explore? Or do you want to make a difference by helping build an orphanage in Guatemala?

What is your vision for your life? Having a vision is beyond wanting to have a lot of money. It is about living your values, loving what you do, spending time with your family and friends, and feeling joy, happiness, and fulfillment every day. It's about doing what is important—contributing to something outside of yourself while taking care of your body and soul.

Have you ever looked back on your life and wondered what happened? Where did the time go, and why did your dreams go by unfulfilled? Just like a plant is either growing or dying, you are either moving toward your goal or away from your goal. While some people may have given up on their dreams and settled for a monotonous life of work and little play, there are others who still have a voice whispering that they can be, do, and have more. As Les Brown says, "Don't let your goals, gifts, abilities, dreams, and talents die with you. What are the dreams you never pursued? The talents you never used? You likely have not even scraped the surface of your abilities. You have greatness within you! Greatness is a choice you must make. You have to reach beyond your comfort zone to win."

How can you turn your dreams into goals and take practical steps toward a successful, happy, and fulfilling life? Well, this book is not about mere dreaming. *Step Into Your Vision 2.0* is a collection of inspirational stories combined with practical tools that you can apply right away. These twenty-four leaders will share with you their story and life lessons, showing you how they have achieved their goals—and how you can too! Whether you are on track right now to achieve your goals or you are struggling to figure out how to make it happen, this book can empower and inspire you. Each coauthor highlights goal setting from a unique personal angle. Their stories show that it's possible to step into your vision, no matter where you are today.

Take for instance Pauline Turton, who was told that her youngest son Michael would never be able to read, write, or hold a job. Was this simply his lot in life? Even though for years it felt as if she was knocking her head against the wall, Pauline had a vision, and she refused to give up. Her older son Matthew shares his personal story of how he overcame his learning disabilities with the help of his mother. Not only did she change the future of her own two sons, she has impacted the lives of hundreds of people with her groundbreaking brain development program. Her story no doubt will inspire you to believe in the impossible.

No words could describe the devastation and the intensity of pain Joyce Hack felt when she lost her husband, soul mate, best friend, and the love of her life in a terrible accident. They had just moved to California to pursue their dreams together. With his death, she was left behind with her two young daughters and far from her family and friends. Much like an architect, she had to go back to the drawing board and write out her plans to build a new life. Her chapter will show you how to turn every obstacle into a gift—an opportunity to grow, learn, and become a better and stronger person.

Aurora Wilson is an amazing example of who you can become when you learn to trust and believe in yourself. A victim of abuse and bullying, she grew up with a self-defeated attitude and no self-worth, believing the people around her who said she would not amount to anything, yet she turned her life around.

Tim Scogin shares how to create your vision board, and John Assaraf will expand on the concept of visualization and how to use that concept to take action and move toward your goals every day. He will show you that you can't just sit around looking at your vision board and expect everything to fall out of the sky into your lap. You have to take responsibility for your life.

Step into your Vision 2.0 provides more than inspirational stories. Gerry Werner, an IT expert, shares how you can use technology to be more efficient and effective and how you can prevent your vision from crashing. Sigrid McNab's chapter teaches powerful strategies to tame your time suckers and become more productive while Dr. Laurén Laurino explains how you can build a business from your passion, allowing you to live the lifestyle you desire.

This is just a small sampling of what lies in store for you in the pages of this book. Each one of the authors is excited to share with you the secrets that have worked for them. Many of them have dealt with tremendous challenges and setbacks, yet somehow they each found a way to get back and continue on the path.

Know that you are not alone on your journey. Each one of the twenty-four inspirational authors is there to support you. If you resonate with someone's story, feel free to contact him or her. We all would love to hear from you! (And when you have an inspirational, empowering story yourself, email me at Shamayah@ coauthorswanted.com.)

It is the foremost hope of all of us that you will create an incredible life and *Step Into **Your** Vision*.

– Shamayah & Coauthors

P.S. If you have enjoyed reading this book, we would appreciate it greatly if you could write a great review on Amazon.com.

CHAPTER I

Cappuccino in Amsterdam

By Shamayah Sarrucco

> *"A boat is safest in the harbor.*
> *But this is not the purpose of a boat."* - *Paulo Coelho*

"Hey, Kyana, so great to see you!"

Mr. J.'s welcome always made Kyana feel loved and cherished—the kind of feeling one got after a big hug and a grand thank you. It was a beautiful spring day. As it's often cloudy and rainy in the Netherlands and sunny days are so rare, the terraces all over the city were crowded with people who didn't want to miss out on the opportunity to catch a few rays of sunshine. The terrace of Café De Jaren was located on one of the many canals that Amsterdam is famous for, dug in the 17th Century during the Dutch Golden age, allowing merchandise from all over the world to be brought to the doorstep of every canal-side merchant. The boats passing under the bridge, and the many bicycles crossing over the bridge, made the view very engaging.

They savored a cup of cappuccino and ate real Dutch apple pie as they caught up on life. Mr. J. could tell that Kyana was worried and something was on her mind. He asked, "Do you remember when you were a little girl and everything was possible? Do you recall the feeling of having dreams with no limits and there were no boundaries to who you could become? You bounced off the walls excited if you had a new brilliant idea for your life. What happened? When did you get so serious?"

"Me? Serious?" Kyana replied.

"You know exactly what I'm talking about, Kyana," Mr. J. said with a smile on his face, saying that she knew she couldn't fool him.

"Well, it's just that my life isn't really what I envisioned it to be. My goal was to buy my own place, and I did. I love my condo. The location is perfect. There are nice restaurants and cafés close by, and the Dam is only twenty minutes away on my bike. I even have a back garden, which is very unique in Amsterdam, because there are so many people living on this little 'stamp.'"

"Achieving your goals is important to finding happiness—we are designed that way. But only if your goals are in alignment with your true purpose will you experience the joy of achieving them." Mr. J. understood the feeling of being trapped living a life of doing what others expect of you very well. He was born in a very wealthy and well-respected family, but he was not the kind of person to sit in college for a boring four years and then follow in his father's footsteps and take over the family business. As a

young man, he wanted to experience life firsthand—to discover what was beyond the river bend, to explore faraway countries, to taste the multicultural culinary experiences, and to make friends with people from around the world.

Even though his family disapproved of his decision, at the age of eighteen, he packed his backpack and his guitar, took his savings out of his bank account, and drove in his BMW from his town Uz in Arabia through Egypt, Libya, Tunisia, and Algeria to Morocco. By the time he made it to Spain and had lived there for several months in a fancy penthouse, he had run out of cash and had to sell his BMW, but he didn't mind. He simply hitchhiked from there. After traveling through Europe, he eventually landed in Amsterdam and built his own wealth. Now he was an old man who enjoyed sharing his wisdom with others. He was a great mentor and dear friend to Kyana. Little did she know that Mr. J. had a much bigger vision in store for her. He had told her on more than occasion that she was using less than 1% of her ability and was capable of so much more, but she had a hard time accepting it. Now he was about to send her on a mission that, if successful, would allow Kyana to impact the lives of millions of people. But if she failed, she might have to pay with her life.

To make sure his words sank in, Mr. J. repeated his earlier words, "Achieving your goals is important to find happiness, but only if your goals are in alignment with your purpose will you experience the true joy of achieving them."

"Is that why I feel like I'm running in a hamster wheel?" Kyana

sighed. "I have a job, but I don't know if I want to keep it. I wish I could do something that would make more of a positive impact on the world. Now it's almost like I'm selling my body for money. But if I quit, I'm afraid for the consequences if I can't pay my mortgage."

"Worrying won't do you any good, my dear. The more serious you get, the more you limit yourself. You know the song, 'Don't Worry, Be Happy,' right? Well, let me tell you: life *really* works that way. You have to be willing to win or lose with the same level of enthusiasm. Did I tell you the story, Kyana, of when I was in South France?"

Kyana knew whenever Mr. J. asked a question like that, there was a valuable lesson to learn. "I would like to hear it," Kyana responded.

"We had hitchhiked from France and ended up somewhere in the countryside because I fell asleep in the back of the truck. My plan was to get back to the main road so I could earn money in Toulouse. There were very few cars coming by on this dirt road, so I walked and walked and walked until I noticed a little house that seemed to be abandoned in the distance. I was tired and decided to check it out. It was a very simple home. There wasn't much, but it was better than sleeping in the grass. There was a bed and a table with two wooden chairs. It was great until I ran out of food after a couple of days. I had found some berries, but that didn't work well for my dog. I didn't know what to do."

He paused for a moment and then continued, "The sun was shining, and worrying wasn't going to do me any good. I got my guitar and started playing. Suddenly, I heard the sound of something

moving toward me from the bushes…crunch…crunch… I stopped playing to hear it better, but then the movement stopped, and the sound was gone. I started playing again, and I could hear whatever it was coming closer and closer. A part of me was getting a little nervous. I hadn't researched what kinds of dangerous animals could be out there. I wondered if it could have been a snake.

"As I kept playing, suddenly I saw a head come out of the bushes. It was a tortoise! I thought 'Great! There's our dinner!' When he was close enough, I grabbed him and found a bag to put him in. Then I continued playing. Again I heard the sound… crunch…crunch… Sure enough, another tortoise found his way out of the bushes, curious to discover where the music was coming from. I caught him too. After playing for an hour or so, I had caught four of them. Then I thought to myself, 'How do you prepare a tortoise? The shell is very hard to crack…'"

"What did you do?" Kyana asked curiously. "If he pulls in his head, there's not much meat."

"True." Mr. J. smiled. "That's why I took the two bags with the turtles, walked to the main road, and got a ride to the city. In Toulouse, I went to the pet store and sold all four of them. Then I had money to buy dog food and get myself some real food as well."

"Did you make this story up, Mr. J?" Kyana laughed.

"No, it is a true story. It taught me that worry is a choice. Worry doesn't allow you to be happy, so it's not a smart choice. You have to take charge and direct your thoughts. Worrying doesn't get you anywhere; it keeps you stuck and sucks you in."

Even though she had known Mr. J. now for years, Kyana was still surprised that he had so many incredible stories to tell and how much she could learn from them.

"Loosen up, girl! You'll be amazed how miracles will happen when you stop being so serious." Mr. J. laughed. "If things don't work out with your job, we can always go hunting for tortoises together. I'm better with my guitar now than I was back in the days. Who knows? We may catch some deer."

Mr. J. continued, "Now on a 'serious' note, there is something I have to share with you." He handed her a card:

A woman precious to many,

Filled with dreams and hopes that will never be

A life too young to be gone:

Our world will never be the same

With great sadness in our hearts,

We say goodbye of our dear friend, sister & daughter

"She was only thirty-five years old. They say she 'fell' out of the window by accident. All her life she had been fighting to make her dreams come true. She had a big vision for her life. Despite the psychologist, psychiatrists, and all the many therapies she tried, her past kept hunting her. She had read the books, attended the seminars, and studied the home study courses, but they didn't give her the real

tools and the right knowledge. She had reached the point where her desperation exceeded her faith. All she wanted was to be happy. I wish I could have helped her, but I only knew the first digit of the code, and it wasn't enough to save her." Mr. J. said.

"That's terrible—such a sad story. But what do you mean by 'the first digit of the code,' Mr. J?" Kyana asked curiously. "The code to what?"

"The world holds the code to the vault that contains the exact formula to find happiness. In my travels, I discovered that achieving goals are critically important if you want to be happy, and those goals need to be in alignment with your true purpose. But I didn't find all the answers. One time, I met an old Maasai woman. The Maasai tribe she belonged to live in the vast plains of the Serengeti in Tanzania, and she told me that unlocking the code would change the world. She was very well-known for her wisdom, and people would travel from all over to ask her advice. I didn't think too much of it until I met a sheik in Arabia three years later. He told me that his great-grandfather had dedicated his life to unlocking the code because his greatest desire was to change the world. But he strangely disappeared before he had been able to share his discoveries. By reading letters his great-grandfather had sent to his dad, the sheik had found the one digit he shared with me:

Don't take life too serious! Play and have fun!

You have to win or lose with the same level of enthusiasm.

"Kyana, you need to find the code. Think about the impact this will have on the world. Many people are overwhelmed with despair and frustration because there is so much wrong information that puts people on the wrong track. I am just too old to travel. I have to warn you though—it's not an easy mission. It will be dangerous. The majority of the people will support you on your mission, but a very few evil, ruthless people with bad intentions will want to take you down."

Mr. J. knew that Kyana was very able to fulfill this important mission, but he also knew that she could not succeed if she didn't have confidence in herself.

Deep in her heart, Kyana knew that her life's purpose was bigger than what she was living right now. She had this burning desire to discover what makes somebody really happy. Ever since she was a little girl, she had observed people, wondering what the recipe was to happiness. She had experienced deep sadness herself, and there had been times that she had felt so miserable— even though on the outside, her life had looked wonderful. Taking on this challenge would mean leaving her family, her friends, and everything she was used to.

"Another cappuccino for you?" The waitress startled her in her thoughts.

"Can I have a fresh orange juice instead please?" Kyana answered, a little absent.

"For you, sir?" The waitress turned to Mr. J.

"Yes please."

As the waitress left, Mr. J. continued the conversation. "Why are you doubting, Kyana?"

"Well, I don't think I can afford to travel right now," she answered. "My job gives me security, and I have a regular paycheck coming in. I need to pay my mortgage, and I don't have enough savings to last me for a very long time. It's not like you're talking about a two-week vacation. This is a really big step. It would probably be best if I save money first. I'd be in a much better position. Hopefully, the market will go up, and I can use the equity of my condo to cover my expenses. Plus, I don't play guitar, Mr. J. How could I catch tortoises? I would starve to death," Kyana said.

"That is exactly how 98% of people think. They wait for the perfect scenario to happen. In the end, most people die before they've ever lived. You can always find an excuse if you're looking for one. Most people don't even consider the journey because they're afraid, and then they justify why they didn't want to go anywhere in the first place. A job doesn't give security—it's a big bubble that can burst at any time. Security can be found in who you become." He paused. "Just imagine how many lives you'll be able to touch. The fulfillment you'll find will surpass the wealth of the earth."

Kyana thought about her job. It had become a monotonous routine, and the meaningless conversations of her coworkers during lunch had made her wonder many times if there was more to life than this.

Mr. J. left money on the table to pay the bill and handed her an envelope. "Here, take this with you. It's some words to ponder. Meet me here tomorrow at noon and we'll talk." He unlocked his bike; and as he drove away, he yelled, "Tomorrow at noon! Don't be late!"

She stood there wondering what to do. She wasn't even sure what to think. Mr. J. had given her valuable advice over the last months, only this time she had her doubts. It sounded like an exciting challenge. There were many obstacles to overcome, but there was much to gain. Continuing to do what she had been doing would be much easier; but then again, there wasn't much fulfillment in it. She unlocked her bike and walked next to it toward the Dam, the famous town square in Amsterdam that jostles with locals, tourists, and pigeons day and night. It was created in the 13th century when a dam was built around the river Amstel to prevent the Zuiderzee Sea from swarming the city. During the sixties, the square was renowned for its Dam Square hippies, and the laid back and relaxed character lives on in this multi-cultural city. Add to that the many tourists that cross the Dam, and you have a fascinating mingle of every continent of the globe. As Kyana walked by the Dam she saw a Japanese couple trying to figure out where they were on the map, an African lady in a colorful, traditional dress calming down her screaming three-year-old son who was scared of the pigeons, a Surinam man walking slowly with a cane, and giggling teenage girls carrying bags of new clothes from their successful shopping

spree. Three Chinese girls were taking pictures of the beautiful Royal Palace. Built in the 17th century, this grand palace was no longer home to the Dutch Royal Family, but it was still used occasionally to hold official receptions. Without a doubt, it was the main attraction of the Dam Square.

Looking at the variety of people, Kyana pondered the idea of traveling and finding the true answers that would unlock the "vault of happiness." She noticed that regardless of where the person was from, their looks, their clothes, or their outward appearance, there was something about their attitude that was similar—something that almost made them seem as if they weren't really alive. She vaguely remembered seeing a book at the bookstore that talked about the emotional tone scale and how it related to our happiness. She made a mental note to buy the book. Then she wondered how many people she could touch if she would take on Mr. J.'s challenge.

It was starting to get dark, so she decided to go home. After preparing a nice chicken salad, she sat down at the kitchen table and suddenly realized that she had not yet opened the envelope that Mr. J. had given her at the café. The golden envelope looked very unique, especially since it had an official seal on it. It was pretty. In fact, if she thought had she not been so curious to find out what was inside, she would have just put it on her chimney as an ornament. She carefully opened the envelope. There was a beautiful card inside that read:

Desire. Design. Destiny.

Like an eagle has the desire to fly,

His design reveals his destiny.

If he were to walk, afraid of heights,

He could never live his purpose.

It's time to live your purpose.

To follow the desire of your heart,

To honor the design of your Creator,

To step into your destiny.

Wow! What powerful words! It made so much sense now. Thinking back on her life, Kyana realized that some of the goals she had achieved were goals that were expected of her rather than goals birthed out of her own desires. On the outside, her life was great. She had a wonderful condo, a company car, a steady job, and fun friends. But deep inside, there was a desire burning to become more and have a profound impact on the lives of other people—to truly make a difference.

"Mr. J. is right," she thought to herself. "There is a bigger game to play. The stakes are high, and so is the reward. I've seen how despair and frustration has zapped the life force out of several friends. I may not know how I'm going to this or what it will take,

but I do know WHY I need to find the answers that will unlock the vault to happiness." She took a deep breath, getting herself ready for the big adventure, "It's time to step into my destiny and make a difference in the world."

"Life is not a matter of chance...it is a matter of choice." – Ka

If you are ready to step into your destiny and want to join Kyana on her adventure to find the code to happiness, go to www.HappinessIsaVerbBook.com/join now.

— ABOUT THE AUTHOR —

Shamayah Sarrucco is the founder of World Class Writing, LLC, a company with gifted writers who incorporate their business expertise in books, newsletters, blogs, and other marketing materials. Shamayah's mission is to empower people and help entrepreneurs capture their expertise on paper so they can share their inspirational messages with the world. Shamayah is an international speaker and the author of *Googlicious, Step into Your Vision,* and *The Diamond from Within.* Her next book, *Happiness is a Verb* will be released Spring 2015. www.worldclasswriting.com

CHAPTER 2

Commit Yourself To Excellence

By Mark F. LaMoure

> *"The will to win, the desire to succeed, the urge to reach your full potential... These are the keys that will unlock the door to personal excellence." – Confucius*

*M*y life was great. I was living in beautiful Lake Placid, NY and in pre-med to become a Doctor of Chiropractic. Just before Christmas, my girlfriend Michelle and I invited my best friend Bill to spend a week with us. We had a fantastic time skiing in the Adirondack Mountains of northern New York and eating at gourmet restaurants. We took Bill to the airport at the end of the week, sad that the time had passed so fast, yet grateful for the valuable friendship we shared. Unfortunately, there were no planes departing due to the bad winter weather, so Michelle drove us back home. The road was dangerously icy. Returning home, we were laughing and chatting; happy about the extra time we could spend

together. Suddenly, our van skidded to the other side of the highway, and we were hit broadside by an oncoming car. I heard Michelle screaming, then everything went black.

Back in Montana, the phone rang. "Hello? Is this Mrs. LaMoure?" "Yes, it is," my mother said.

The woman continued, "I am Mark's emergency doctor here at the Adirondack Medical Center. I'm sorry to inform you that your son was in a terrible car accident. He's badly injured and has lacerations, several broken bones, and an injured neck."

"Is he going to be okay?" My mom asked, concerned.

"I wish I had better news for you, Ma'am," the doctor said. "But your son is in a deep coma, and there is less than a 3% chance that he'll survive. I suggest you fly out here as soon as you can."

My mom was shocked and devastated. She wanted to see me very much, but she and my dad were too old and frail to fly. So my caring brother and sister got on the next plane to see me before I died. Michelle and Bill were badly injured as well, but although their injuries were painful, they weren't life-threatening and they were released from the hospital after about two weeks. It was a miracle we were all still alive. The van was a horrible wreck of smashed, twisted steel. Fortunately, I was in very good shape for a twenty-five-year old man. After remaining comatose for a while, the doctors wanted to harvest my organs, as they believed I would die anyway. My parents refused, believing there was still a possibility that I could come back to life – and they were right!

Awakening to Life

Lying in a comatose state was a tough, but incredible experience. After twenty-one days, I unexpectedly awakened from the coma. Waking up was one of the hardest things I've ever done. At first, I was upset. I could hardly move, and it was hard to adjust to what had happened. I had to relearn how to think, talk, and walk. Being disabled was difficult, but I refused to give up. I constantly read, studied, and exercised to improve myself. I worked hard for years to recover, and I never could have done it without God, my family, girlfriend, the medical staff, and good friends. I am very thankful for their support and loving care, and will always appreciate what they did for me.

Life after the car accident was hard, to say the least, because of the physical and emotional pain. Yet the life lessons it taught me were profound. Pain and adversity make you think deeply. The car accident served as a forced education, and it gave me deeper wisdom. In the end, I became a far better person after going through the huge ordeal.

Making Excellence Happen

Life is a do-it-yourself project. A sculptor works to carve something beautiful out of stone. You need to be the sculptor of your life, and carve out the person you want to become. You can carve your unique talents and abilities into something excellent. Do whatever it takes; persistence brings success. Make excellence your motto.

When trials and tribulations happen, praying and working hard can give you what you need. In the beginning, I struggled to exercise and to relearn thinking, reading, and studying. I triumphed over my pain and smiled through life's trials and tribulations. I was determined to get 100% well. I fully recovered from the accident, which is a miracle. To get healthier, I ate super-nutritious food and did weight and strength training. Over the years, I've run hundreds of road races and walked tens of thousands of miles. My dedication to constant reading and studying was also beneficial to me. At Pepperdine University in Malibu, CA, I became a top graduate student in an honors program. I earned graduate scholarships and assistantships. I became a student leader and was elected graduate student president, twice. No matter how hard life gets, you need to remember:

"Even the darkest night ends and the sun will shine."

These are the lessons I've learned. They will help you achieve your goals and overcome any obstacle you may face.

1. Dedicate yourself to being a happy, healthy person regardless of your circumstances.
2. Do something every day that brings you closer to your goals. Write a daily to-do list and take action.
3. Always work hard. Be determined to win. Never give up.
4. Make it a habit to think positive.
5. Act as if it is impossible to fail and be persistent.

Determination To Succeed

A few years later, I launched a nutrition business in network marketing. Everything starts small, no matter how big it becomes later. I had a burning desire to succeed, and I vowed to be a success. My business started to take off the day I purchased *Think And Grow Rich* by Napoleon Hill. My goal was to be outstanding in my business and become an extraordinary leader. After reading that "The greatest among you will be servants to your people," I decided to become excellent at helping others. I trained my network marketing team to be exceptional. Our meetings were held in the meeting rooms of the best restaurants, and I made sure they were highly educational and very fun. My wife and I threw parties at our home to celebrate our people and show them thanks. By inspiring success and cultivating our team with love and care, as well as providing superb training, they blossomed to become excellent business performers. I was very proud of them. In less than a year my commitment to excellence boosted me into the top ten out of hundreds of thousands of distributors worldwide. This continued for years, as I sold nutrition products around the globe.

If you want to step into your vision, you have to dare to dream big.

* Use self-discipline. It is a powerful virtue and promotes success.
* Become an excellent planner. Write down your goals and constantly update them.

* Every day, write a to-do list and take action.
* Work harder and smarter than other people. Strive to deliver excellence.
* Develop great social skills. Learn good manners and be courteous to everyone.
* Be a generous person. Be giving, helpful and compassionate.
* Be a team player.
* It is amazing how much easier you win, by using love for success.

EXCELLENCE

"Now is the right time for you to become excellent. By taking action on your dreams of excellence, you start polishing the rough diamond you are. As you buff and shine yourself with practice, sparkling success becomes yours." – Mark F. LaMoure

Five Action Steps to Become Excellent

Excellence is an essential quality of success. The word *excellence* comes from the word *excel*, meaning "to go beyond the average." It also means "to be remarkable or extraordinary." You are immensely powerful and full of potential. It is never too late to start anew and be what you might have been. With determination, you can become the embodiment of excellence. Work to make excellence your personal trademark. Excellence doesn't mean perfection; it is a result of self-improvement.

Many of the famous and outstanding people I've met are very humble and thankful. The Olympic gold medal winners I know are humble and grateful individuals. We can use them as great examples to learn from. Be confident and show your charisma, but display it with gratitude and humility. This enhances your personal value.

From years of experience, I've discovered secrets that can lift you to success. Put these ideas to work and watch your life grow with exceptional results. The following is a valuable blueprint to develop excellence:

1 **Write down your goals on what you want to be excellent at**. Then write a daily to-do list to guide you, step-by-step, to achieving excellence. Daily planning delivers golden success. Concentrate daily on your goals.

2 **Be determined to become extraordinary.** Write down at least three benefits you will reap by being a person of excellence at what you want. Look for the positive. This will empower and inspire you to achieve success.

3 **Read good books and magazines on topics that inspire excellence**. Take educational courses and workshops for self-improvement to grow your knowledge. Watch TV and movies related to subjects on excellence that you like.

4 **Learn from people you admire.** Pick people with high standards. Aim high. Choose friends who are exceptional. It's

far better to have a few high-quality, golden friendships than a large quantity of superficial friends.

5 **Practice daily, always working a little harder at what you want to be excellent at.** Persistence leads to achievement. Always do more than others do, as this can make you a master.

It's never too late to start being excellent. Self-improvement for excellence is easy. If you improve at least 5% daily five days per week, you'll improve at least 1300% each year. Excellence is a high quality that produces top-level success. Endorse your life with a signature of excellence. Always plan for the future, but take action today. When you do today what others won't, tomorrow you can have what others can't. Your life is what you make it, so commit yourself to excellence.

— ABOUT THE AUTHOR —

Mark F. LaMoure is a one-of-a-kind inspiring author, keynote speaker, and trainer. He is known for his articles, book reviews, and entrepreneurship. As a thought leader, Mark enriches people's lives. He is a multilingual international businessman who has lived in different parts of the world from Brazil to England, and New York to California. Mark inspires people to greatness. He is a visionary speaker who talks with color to groups on excellence, wealth building and success. Find inspiration. Contact Mark F. LaMoure by phone at 1-208-429-9229 or by email at mlamoure@cableone.net. His website is www.MarkLaMoure.com. Read his excellent articles at: Mark F. LaMoure, Author – EzineArticles.com.

CHAPTER **3**

Turning Stumbling Blocks into Stepping Stones

By Pauline Turton

"All things are possible for the one who has faith." – Mark 9:23

itting at the dining room table, I said a silent prayer. If you had looked through the window, you would have seen a perfect picture: A mom sitting at the table with books, notebooks, and pens, homeschooling her sons. I loved my boys, yet it was a daunting task to teach them, because they had major learning disabilities. In addition, they had flaming ADHD. It was overwhelming! My husband and I knew that they were smart; but like a square peg in a round hole, a traditional classroom wasn't the answer. Initially, I thought two or three years of one-on-one attention would prepare them, but I didn't seem to be able to find the keys to unlock the struggles they were dealing with. I prayed daily for the patience and faith to face the challenge.

When Michael was nine years old, two psychologists told us that he would never be able to read, write, or even hold a job. We were given five different diagnoses, which I knew in my heart were accurate. After a very short grieving process, I decided that we couldn't accept that as God's plan for our son. For years I knocked my head against the wall; but I knew if we didn't get the issues in their brains addressed, they would never be able to fulfill what God had planned for them. Every evening I prayed from the depth of my heart, asking God to show me how I could help my sons. Despite my background as a teacher and a psychiatric nurse, combined with years of committed effort, my youngest son still couldn't read a word by the end of third grade, and my oldest son couldn't write more than three sentences after an hour of hard work.

One day stands out clearly in my memory. Michael was going for a playtime with another homeschooler, and he was waiting for me to finish cleaning the kitchen after lunch before taking him to his friend's house for the afternoon. I stood directly in front of him and said, "Come on, Michael. It's time to get your shoes on; we're leaving." I knew he was looking forward to playing with his friend, yet he didn't move. I waited, and waited, and waited, thinking, *'If you don't want to get your shoes, then we just won't go.'* For some reason, I didn't say anything. I just stood there and waited. Eventually, after waiting for a long time, he exclaimed, "Ok, Mom!" and he happily got up to put on his shoes.

I started crying. I realized that it took all that time for his brain to receive and process the information. Prior to this moment, I had

repeated requests like most parents do when their child doesn't seem to be listening. However, our repeating was just jamming the channels in his brain. When I allowed him a longer time to process, he was able to understand. He'd been trying to understand instructions for years, yet he was getting in trouble for things that really weren't his fault. His brain hadn't received the information, causing him to become angry and frustrated. This was an eye-opening moment, as it helped me to look at our situation from a new perspective. Now I knew we needed to find a way to speed up his brain's processing time—and for now, we needed to stop repeating requests! It was an emotional moment realizing that I had an expectation he couldn't possibly fulfill. The 30 seconds, which felt like hours, I waited in silence for Michael to get his shoes, gave me a new perspective on Michael's listening challenges.

Rather than just looking at the academic skills it takes to learn, I started thinking, "What skills in the brain have to be operating in order for a child to learn?" In nursing school, we were told that the heart can regroup and recover if it had a small damaged spot, but the brain could not. I remember wondering that day, "Why would God make our heart able to recover but not give our brain that same ability?" I decided to challenge the traditional thinking. Instead of trying to break down a concept into what I thought were digestible pieces, I headed out in a new direction looking for ways to develop the brain's abilities underneath learning—things like memory skills. This decision took my journey in a completely different direction.

After seven years of researching everything I could about the brain, talking to brain experts, and praying and working with my children, I woke up one morning with the revelation, *"The brain is like a set of muscles."* When I learned to exercise those muscles in an intense way, my children's lives would be impacted forever. That was a major breakthrough! I realized that by exercising specific areas of the brain, they could be trained. Shortly after my breakthrough, I met two mentors who believed this was possible. We studied the work of Dr. Guilford, Elizabeth Allen MA, Dr. Mary and Dr. Robert Meeker (Structure of Intellect), Dr. Jerome Rosner, and several others. I learned to develop the underlying brain skills needed to be successful in academics.

In Michael's case, one of the brain skills he needed strengthened was his short-term memory. He could only remember things for approximately three seconds. He was consistently forgetting what he was supposed to do, just like Dory from *Finding Nemo*. For instance, I would send him to the basement to get a can of fruit from the cellar, and he either wouldn't come back because he forgot he'd been sent, or he would come back asking what he was supposed to do. This was one of the reasons he couldn't learn to read. He couldn't remember a short word for even a few seconds. He had great difficulty forming letters, and they were often reversed. He also had serious speech and eye tracking problems, the auditory lag mentioned earlier, as well as auditory discrimination issues. (His brain didn't register all of the sounds within words—some sounds were overheard, and others were barely recorded at all.)

Finally! This concept of exercising, and therefore developing, brain skills would change the outcome of my boys' lives and help them reach their potential! The results were profound. Today, Michael enjoys reading and can do so at an adult level with good comprehension. One of his gifted areas is working with his hands. He works full time in construction—dry walling, roofing, replacing windows, etc. He enjoys all kinds of people and likes to help them solve problems.

Matthew, who has his own chapter in this book, used to follow nine different trains of thought all at once, therefore he couldn't focus on any one thought successfully. He had memory issues as well as dysgraphia. His hand would pain after writing a few words, and he had great difficulty forming letters. He struggled with Expressive Language Disorder (written format). He had lots of ideas, but he couldn't organize them or put them on paper. By the time he was 15 years old, he still could only write three sentences in an hour of hard work. After an assessment, we discovered two skills required for written language were disabled, but his overall abilities were in the gifted range. We needed to exercise those two skills until they were strong enough to balance and integrate with his other skills. We had that breakthrough on January 25th of his tenth grade year. Four days later, he went to school for the first time after being homeschooled for ten years. He managed a full course load, including English and History (which require the most writing). He graduated from college with an Early Childhood Education diploma with no accommodations. He is completing

his third year of university toward a psychology degree with an average of 87%. Ironically, many of his projects are essays. He is now the Vice President of Breakthroughs in Learning and Careers.

Our belief that God had a plan for our children kept us from giving up and accepting the "verdict" from the psychologists. Our sons' lives were impacted in a big way. I really do believe that all things are possible for those who have faith. My husband and I prayed all the way through this journey, and I believe that God had a bigger plan than I could imagine at the time. We've been able to impact and improve the lives of thousands of adults, teens, and children by helping them develop the brain skills needed to be more successful in life. These are some of the powerful lessons I learned along the way:

* **The gift of prayer** - Believe that anything is possible and that God can give you answers. Have faith in the Creator. Many times I'd go to bed in desperation praying for guidance because I needed information that only the Creator knew. The next morning, I'd wake up with a new idea that sometimes sounded completely crazy, but it was a clue that helped me to understand that the brain has the God-given ability to change, grow, and adapt.

* **The power of persistence** - You have to decide that you're going to do whatever it takes, no matter how long it takes. Growing up, my parents always said, "Where there's a will, there's a way," and "If at first you don't succeed, try, try again." Those words were deeply ingrained in my life. Never give up and have an open mind to look at your situation from

a new perspective if what you've been doing is not creating the results you want. Sometimes your training and your knowledge can limit your ability to see new strategies. In my case, I had to change my perspective by setting aside what I had learned as a teacher and in psychiatric nursing to get different results.

❋ **The value of working together** - It is very important to have goals as a family and to have open conversations about how you are going to achieve them. We all had to make sacrifices. When our sons' grandparents died, we inherited money. We sat our boys down and explained to them that we could set the money aside in a college fund. However, if things didn't change, going to college wasn't very viable for them. Instead, we could invest this money in trying to find answers as to how we could help make learning easier for them. We made the right choice.

When I started talking with other parents eighteen years ago about the ability of the brain to develop, they looked at me as if I was from outer space. Even though it's more widely known today, there are many teachers, doctors, and parents who are totally unaware that the brain can be developed. Parents spend money on tutoring, which involves teaching content, because they want their child to succeed, but they often see limited or temporary improvement. Tutoring takes a concept and breaks it into smaller chunks so that the child might understand it more easily. That is exactly what I was doing the first four years, but it didn't help my

children. For example, if a child doesn't have sufficient memory or listening comprehension levels, it doesn't matter how many steps you break the process into; the child simply doesn't remember and/or comprehend it. That's why it is critically important that a child develops the brain skills underneath learning in order to be successful long term. We develop brain skills by training them at a level that is easy for the child to perform. That way the "muscle strength" can gradually increase. We have all kinds of clients today—including those with different types of autism, to every kind of learning disability you can imagine.

Last week, I met a young girl who is very bright, but she doesn't have long-term memory retrieval. She studies and understands the material; but when it is time to take the test a couple of days later, she can't recall the answers. It is very frustrating for her because she studies and understands the material, yet her grades don't reflect her effort. Probably 90% of the children and adults who come to our office have memory issues.

We also often see weak judgment skills in children. When this area is weaker than expected for the age of the child, it can lead to poor decision making. For example, a three-year-old does what he is being told without questioning or discerning whether something is appropriate. As adults, we understand and accept that behavior from a three-year-old, but we have different expectations from a ten-year-old. So if a ten-year-old has the judgment skills of a three-year-old, he often gets in trouble. This is frustrating for both the child and the parents.

If you or your child is struggling to learn, know that change and success are possible. I encourage you to take action. Don't wait! Chronic failure dramatically affects self-esteem, produces behavioral problems, and causes resistance to education. For more information about how you can get your breakthrough, visit www.GetYourBreakthrough.com/warning-signs and get your free copy of the Warning Signs Checklist.

— ABOUT THE AUTHOR —

Pauline's teaching experience and extensive work in the field of psychiatry prompted her to research the brain's restorative capabilities. Pauline is the mother of two sons who have overcome significant learning disabilities. After years of research, she built Breakthroughs in Learning to provide hope and help through educational therapy. Over the last nineteen years, Pauline has helped thousands of children and families. As a conference speaker and workshop leader, Pauline continues to share the wealth of knowledge she has gained during her journey. Contact her at (519) 888-6697 or pauline@getyourbreakthrough.com or visit her website at www.GetYourBreakthrough.com

From Torment to Triumph

By Matthew Turton

> *"The difference between stumbling blocks and stepping stones is how you use them." – Tom Sims*

*a*s a kid growing up with three learning disabilities, failure was no stranger to me. My parents did their best to hide it and shelter me, but I knew—deep down, I knew I was a failure. It didn't matter that everyone else thought I was smart and intelligent; I knew I was different. When I was four years old, I refused to write my name like everyone else who'd put their names on their craft so the Sunday school teacher would know whose it was. When my mom asked about it, I told her, "Don't worry, Mom, she knows that the only one without a name on it is mine!"

Just imagine how it would feel to be a nine-year-old boy, sitting at your desk. No matter how hard you try, you can't write and you

can't focus. As a little kid, I thought something was wrong with my pencil because the words just wouldn't pour óut like they did for the other kids. It didn't take long to realize my *pencil* wasn't the problem.

As adults, we are pretty good at avoiding situations that make us look bad; but as a child, your weaknesses are easily exposed when you can't keep up with the rest of the class. Every child expects to be successful when he starts school. Some become withdrawn, while others act out when they have learning disabilities that prevent them from succeeding.

It was obvious from a young age that my brother and I wouldn't do well in a traditional classroom. According to a local mental health hospital, I was the worst case of ADHD they had ever seen. I also had dysgraphia, which made writing extremely difficult to the point of physical pain. My brother had five diagnoses and two psychologists had predicted that he would never read, write, or have a job. My mother knew that unless things dramatically changed, neither one of us would be able to function in the world, so she decided to homeschool us. Despite her background as a teacher and a psychiatric nurse, homeschooling my brother and I was not an easy task because neither of us was able to concentrate. Every night she would pray for guidance about how to help us succeed in life. Her faith and determination that we would have a better future gave her courage and patience to persist.

With the last of my brother's diagnoses and being told there was no existing help for our extreme challenges, my mother launched

into seven years of research looking for answers, traveling North America, and consulting and training with doctors, groundbreaking specialists, and experts, while spending thousands of dollars attempting to help us. We did every program you can imagine (and some you can't). My dad took a second job, and mom picked up a part-time job to fund the research. She read every night for 1-3 hours for seven years. When I was ready to give up after another failure, she just pressed on to find the next piece to our puzzle.

Even though I couldn't write, I was a ferocious reader. Every week I would get ten new books from the library. I picked up a book from the shelf one day, and after reading several chapters, I went to find Mom and said, "Mom, I have ADHD."

My mom answered, "I know that, but how do you know?" This was a pivotal moment for me because I realized that I wasn't a freak and that my inability to control myself had a name. Knowing that there were other people with the same problems who were successful gave me hope and determination to find answers. From that day on, my mom and I became a team. Together we learned how to break down the steps that would help me focus and then practice those steps over and over and over again. We worked on the premise that ADHD isn't so much a lack of focus, but it's an inability to *control* the focus. Academics became secondary to developing the foundational skills required for being a successful learner.

It was devastating that at the age of fifteen, it would take me an hour to write three sentences with enormous effort. I didn't have

the skills necessary to organize my thoughts, even though I was very gifted in other areas. Something as simple as cleaning up my room was a big challenge. It was like telling a blind person, "Just open your eyes and look around." If you don't have the skill, you just can't do it. Every day my mom would practice with me to specifically target and develop the parts of my brain that were responsible for the dysgraphia and Expressive Language Disorder (my inability to write). It required a lot of patience, determination, and persistence on both our parts.

There are moments in life that seem frozen in time—your first bike, your first kiss, your wedding, holding your first child, and other such events. January 25, 1999, was a momentous day in my life! That day I wrote a full page in fifteen minutes. That day I had my breakthrough! Our home exploded with celebration, tears, and relief. It had happened! I could do it! The last seven years of dedication had finally paid off. It was worth it after all!

Now that I could write, my parents enrolled me in school. I successfully completed Grade 10 without accommodations and without the teachers knowing anything about my past learning challenges. I requested this because I didn't want to just squeak by and find out later that they were just passing me along. It was hard work, but while carrying a full course load I got 72% and 74% in English and History – the courses with the most writing. We had a pizza party to celebrate!

Looking back, I remember when I was eleven years old and nearly six feet tall, Mom and I had spent an exhausting day

looking for new pants. After an unsuccessful shopping trip, my mom decided to splurge and actually take me *out* for lunch. She asked me if I had any idea what I wanted to do when I grew up. Just thinking about that moment still chokes me up. I looked at her and I said, "Mom, I want to do what you do, because someone needs to tell kids they're not stupid."

And so my life path was set. It took seven years of persistent practice before I was able to control my focus. At first I did it by squeezing a ball in my pocket, but later I was able to attend three-hour psychology lectures at a university and run our company—without the ball. I learned to develop the parts of the brain that were responsible for the dysgraphia and Expressive Language Disorder (the inability to write), and now I receive 85 to 98% in my writing assignments at the University of Waterloo.

As the Vice President of Breakthroughs, I am doing exactly what I had envisioned as an eleven-year-old boy: I help children realize they are *not* dumb and they *can* succeed. I speak at teacher conferences and help parents understand that every child can succeed by developing the right brain skills.

There are five important lessons I learned on my journey that I'd like to share with you:

1 **It's not your fault:** Some things in life we have no control over. Blaming yourself or God keeps you focused on the problem. Instead, you need to shift your focus to the solution. It is what it is, so what are you going to do about it?

2 **Some people may not get it:** We see the world through the functioning of our own brains and assume that others think the same way. Don't assume your client, spouse, or child has the same skills you do. Something you find easy might be soul-crushingly difficult for them.

3 **Your abilities don't define who you are:** Despite a high IQ, excellent verbal skills, and an assessment by a psychologist placing me in the gifted range, every time an assignment or test required writing it was a guaranteed "F." I wasn't stupid, but I was unable to express my intelligence in the way that society expects. We all have strengths and weaknesses—acknowledge both, but don't accept your weakness as permanent.

4 **Trying harder doesn't always help:** It doesn't matter how hard you try to lift 500 pounds—it's probably not going to happen. In fact, you'll probably snap like a twig. If your skill is too weak to be successful in an area, just trying harder isn't going to help. You may need to look at the problem from a different perspective, or you may need to develop strength by starting with less weight and gradually build your muscles.

5 **Find the real cause of the problem:** Instead of looking for ways to avoid an area of weakness, tackle it head on. Discover what level you can successfully function at and develop the underlying skills. For example, when you are trying to learn the multiplication tables, weak memory skills may be the reason it's difficult. Therefore memory skills need to be

developed first. You will see far better growth and development exercising your brain at the level of success than at the point of failure.

Your brain is incredible! Just the fact that you are reading these words is lighting up vast portions of your brain. Science has finally caught up to the point where we can literally watch our brains grow, change, and develop. And the best part is that it doesn't have to take you nearly as long as it took me. Every brain has areas of strength and weakness. What are you going to do with your weaknesses? Will they be stumbling blocks or stepping stones? The choice is up to you!

If you or your child is struggling to learn, know that change and success are possible. Take action—don't wait! Waiting won't produce different results. Chronic failure dramatically affects self-esteem, causes behavioral problems, and produces resistance to education. For more information about how you can get your breakthrough, visit www.GetYourBreakthrough.com/warning-signs and get your free copy of the Warning Signs Checklist.

— ABOUT THE AUTHOR —

As a child who struggled to overcome learning disabilities himself, Matthew Turton always knew he wanted to help other children learn that they weren't stupid. Now an Educational Therapist and Vice President of Breakthroughs in Learning & Careers, he has worked over 15,000 hours with children and adults with learning disabilities. He shares the experience and wealth of knowledge he has gained during his journey as conference speaker and workshop leader. Visit his website at www.GetYourBreakthrough.com or email him at matthew@getyourbreakthrough.com.

CHAPTER 5

Designing Your Destiny

By Karen Orell

> *"Destiny is not a matter of chance, but of choice. Not something to wish for, but to attain."* - William Jennings Bryan

*E*ver since I was a little girl, I loved ballet, tap, and the artistic world. In fact, I've always had a passion for creative expression and design, so I trained and immersed myself in all kinds of artistic endeavors. It was my lifelong dream to become a fashion designer. That vision was always so clear that I felt it would happen no matter what. Despite earning a degree from the Fashion Institute of Design and Merchandising and working in Los Angeles doing costume design, my destiny ended up on a different path.

After struggling for months to pay my bills as an LA designer, an opportunity to make a substantial income arose. Instead of staying true to my heart and my love of art and design, I shifted to

a career in consumer electronics. That decision changed the course of my entire life. For the next eighteen years, I owned a number of successful companies in the high-tech industry. I enjoyed many aspects of the businesses, but I also felt unfulfilled at times, missing my artistic outlets. After many years of wondering why I wasn't fulfilled when I had such great business success, I realized it was my lack of creative outlets. I began working on balancing this by adding creative expression time into my schedule. I volunteered at my children's school teaching art classes, did costume design at local theaters, and took unique painting classes. By adding these avenues of artistic endeavors I was able to find more joy in everything I did.

The Lesson I Want to Share

Stay focused on your passion, especially when amazing opportunities arise, or even when obstacles have you take a different road. If you have allowed distractions to get you sidetracked from your true destiny, and you now realize that the decisions you've made didn't create the life you wanted, just remember it's not too late to change your course. Following your passion is worth more than anything money can give you. Money can definitely make things a lot easier and more enjoyable; but in the long run, money won't fulfill your deepest desires to become all you can be and to live your destiny.

Very few people focus on their loves and passions. Most small business owners and professionals have chosen a career or business

that focuses first on "making a lot of money" instead of the path that is most in alignment with their gifts and joys. You may have done this as well. Unfortunately, I've made the same mistake at various times in my life. Once I became aware of the sacrifice I was making by not doing what I love, I made a shift. I became a business coach, and I love working with artistic entrepreneurs as a great outlet for my own creative expression.

"The only person you are destined to become is the person you decide to be." - Ralph Waldo Emerson

Getting Clear

When you truly express who you are and are passionate about what you do, then your life will be more joyful and productive. Opportunities will come your way effortlessly. The most amazing thing about fully expressing your passion is that it's very evident to others in just your presence and energy. When you are clear on who you are, others will be drawn to you because they see and appreciate your skills and talents!

Exercise for Successful Planning

Being proactive by planning is a major key in achieving what is truly important to you. To get started with your planning, you need to be very clear that your goals are expressed from your heart—that you are truly passionate about them. There are a number of areas to investigate to help you be more clear and focused on your life goals

and on achieving them—they are your joys, gifts, motivators, and most significantly, your life mission. I've designed some effective and easy techniques that work to gain clarity. Take time to sit with your answers, even over a few days and explore them fully.

What are your true joys in life?

One of the key factors to achieve your greatest life is being "in the flow." Being in the flow is like having the optimum use of your physical form to direct your energy into the goals you have for your life. The clearer you are on what your true joys are, the more you'll be able to contribute to the world around you—and in turn, the happier you'll be.

Exercise for Pinpointing Your Greatest Joys in Life
What you'll need:
* Set up a two-hour window without interruption
* Quiet location
* Journal and pen

1 **Block out two hours on your calendar for complete solitude and privacy.** The best time will usually be first thing in the morning or later in the evening when your mind is best able to clear other daily activities out. A weekend day off is another good choice since you're not usually as committed to other activities or appointments on the weekend.

2 **Decide on a location that you find especially peaceful and nurturing.** A great choice is somewhere in nature where

you feel especially happy and content. One of my favorite locations is a glider port overlooking the Pacific Ocean where I can really have a great high-level vantage point. A location like this with a view will help with more long-term thinking and with a greater overall view of your life.

3 **Find a comfortable place to sit and center yourself by closing your eyes and doing deep breathing for about five minutes.** Relax your entire body as you breathe and bring your focus into your center and your heart.

4 **Beginning at your birth,** Start To Slowly Review Your Life Looking For The Most Joyful And Exciting Moments That You Ever Experienced. Moments where time stood still and you were in complete bliss will stand out for you as landmarks. Notice who you are with, your surroundings, and what part of the event you found exciting and fulfilling.

5 **As these events come to mind, write down the feelings you had at that time.** Add notes on everything at that event that contributed to those feelings.

6 **After you finish writing these, look at the common themes of people, locations, and activities.** Finding these common themes will give you a major foundation for planning your life including where you live, what type of work you do, and who you're in relationships with.

The optimal situation would be to produce an income doing the activities you find most fun and exciting. If that's not the case right now, find other ways to include these activities in your daily life.

What gifts and talents do you have to offer?

Determining and clarifying your gifts and talents is like a road map for your life. This exercise can help you find your strengths.

Exercise for Finding Your Gifts and Talents

The people who know you best are a great source of information about who you are at your deepest levels. Select six to ten friends, relatives, or close business associates for feedback. You can tell them that you are working on a project. Ask them the following questions:

1. If you were to describe me to someone who doesn't know me, what would you say?
2. What words come to mind when you think of me?
3. How would you describe my personality?
4. What do you see as my greatest strengths?

Create a list of the words, phrases and traits they give you. Find the common words, personality traits, and themes. Write a list of the top five of each of these. Once you have written down your answers to the exercises, use them as the foundation to set your goals. Then use this new clarity to choose the right livelihood and income producing activities that will truly fulfill your destiny. You could use the words and phrases from the previous exercise in your

bio, resume, or promotional materials for your business. Using the words, phrases and themes discovered through this exercise will allow the written material you present to others to be a clear reflection of who you are.

Even though my eighteen years in the high-tech world were a major turn in my road of life—completely different from what I originally planned—I gained an amazing amount of business knowledge and experience that now supports my own business as well as thousands of other people with their businesses. My intuitive and creative talents have been balanced with business skills in a way that allows for the administrative and operational side of the business to run smoothly, the sales and marketing side to thrive, and the artistic and development side of the business to blossom. If you've spent many years doing something you didn't plan to do or didn't prefer, take time now to acknowledge and write down the assets and skills you gained from that experience. Be thankful for the knowledge you gained from these experiences. It is all an important part of who you are now and what you have to offer.

My Karenism on Goal Setting:
"If you don't know where you're going,
how will you know when you get there?"

Your Vision & Goal Setting

By having the information you've gathered in these exercises, you can create a mission statement for your life and set clear goals. You now have your own list of joys, gifts, and personality traits that can act as your compass in both your personal and business life.

Seven Areas of Your Life

There are seven key areas of your life that are important to have clarity on in order to achieve your goals and have a balanced life:

Your Inner Game
* Spiritual
* Physical
* Mental
* Emotional

Your Outer Game
* Relationships
* Finances
* Community

Write your new set of goals for each of these seven areas for short-term (90 days), mid-term (2-5 years), and long-term goals (lifetime) you want to achieve. Now prioritize the goals you have written and focus on the top three in each area.

Staying on Track with your Goals

Daily track your progress. Post your long-term goals in a place you see every day to remind you of what is important and what you want to see manifest in your life. Share your goals with your community to get support and help you stay on track. Revisit your long-term goals at least once a month to see if they need revision, and revise your goals as needed. I like to do a revisit of my goals at the beginning of each new month and start every new month with a clear plan. Be sure to reward yourself for accomplishing a goal. This will reinforce goals as being important and keep you excited about accomplishing them.

By being really clear on *the* most important thing, you'll stay focused and achieve success. You can make decisions that lead to the expression of your highest self. As choices come up, ask yourself, "Does this get me closer to my goal?" If it doesn't, you will most assuredly do better by making a different choice. If you do this consistently, you'll see your goals realized in your life because you won't allow room for distraction.

Being clear about what is most important to me and having clear, focused goals has allowed me to return to what I love by incorporating my passion into my business. By choosing clients in creative fields like artists, musicians, and designers, I get the opportunity to express my love of design and the creative arts. This has been wonderfully fulfilling and exciting for me.

Find a way to balance your true love with creating financial success in your own life and create the life of your dreams! Be

clear on who you are and why you are here. At every opportunity, make the choices that lead to your greatest self. *Design Your Own Destiny* and take great joy in the life you've created.

Get your special free gift for readers of this book at www.KarenOrell.com/Free-Gift.

— ABOUT THE AUTHOR —

Karen Orell is an international speaker, author, and leader whose life-changing expertise has touched the lives of thousands through her radio shows, television appearances, travel tours, and live events. She inspires, mentors, and empowers entrepreneurs and business professionals to achieve and live their greatest dreams, shifting their lives and the lives of all those they touch, to create a more fulfilled and prosperous global community. To find out more about how Karen can help you realize your dreams and design your own destiny, write her at Karen@KarenOrell.com or visit her website www.KarenOrell.com.

CHAPTER **6**

Taming Your Time Suckers

By Sigrid McNab

> *"Start by doing what's necessary, then do what's possible, and suddenly you are doing the impossible." - Francis of Assisi*

"*M*an!" I groaned to my daughter, my head laying on the desk with my hands clasped to my ears, "I'm so darn frustrated! I'm so sick of all of this stuff I have to do! It's taking me so much longer than everyone else. What takes them half an hour takes me two hours! It seems to take forever to get ahead. I've had it! I need to do something about it!" I had just started my online business, and I had no idea what I was doing. I was tired of struggling, and I was overwhelmed with all the things I had to do. I felt like a runaway train.

In this fast-paced world, life can get pretty crazy. Do you sometimes feel that there are just not enough hours in a day? Are you overwhelmed with the many things on your to-do list?

Would you like to find a better balance? I certainly did. Without a system, it's easy to bob about like a boat in the water with no sail, no motor, and no clarity as to which direction to go. It can be very depressing and discouraging, feeling like you are going nowhere fast. After a while, you can get to the point where you stop believing in yourself because you are not reaching your goals. And if you don't believe in yourself, who will?

This is EXACTLY how I felt that day with my head on the desk. My daughter kept telling me, "Mom, it's okay." Even my dogs came and laid their heads on my lap. So, after I had a good cry, I pulled myself up. I had to stop and take a breath. There had to be a better way to get things done. So, I stepped back and looked at what was going on as if I was an outside observer. Suddenly, this realization came into my head:

"I am 100 % responsible for every area and every circumstance in my life! I am responsible for what I do and for what I should have or could have done but didn't. I am responsible for how I respond to what happens to me."

In that moment, I realized it was all me! When you really understand this, it is so liberating. You can now take ownership! Instead of suffering from self-doubt, you can simply replace bad habits with good habits. That will change your life completely! It did for me. From the frustration I experienced 18 months ago, I started to use a system with new empowering habits—a system

that will help you achieve your goals with less effort and more confidence.

What if there was a way to make your productivity levels soar? What if you could get more accomplished in less time? Wouldn't that be great? This system will help you gain clarity and direction. It will increase your productivity and tame your "time suckers."

Before I explain the process and how you can use it to achieve your goals, it is important for you to know your "why" first. *Why* do you want to reach your goals? In other words, you first have to decide who you want to *be*. Once you understand your inner drive or motivation, it will just make sense to take action every day toward your goals. Remember, your DAILY ACTIONS will determine your long-term success. What are you doing with every minute and every second of your time?

"All men are very much alike. Only their habits separate them. Time is the irretrievable element. The most important choice you will ever make is how you use your time. Remember... every second counts."- Gary Halbert

Being productive is a lot easier said than done, as there are so many distractions. Electronics and gadgets can be wonderful tools to increase productivity, but they can also have the opposite effect and become your biggest distractions. Bright shiny objects can pull you away from the actions that really matter.

You probably don't recognize any of these unproductive habits, do you?

* You are focused on an important project, when you hear "ding" and you stop in the middle of your work to respond to the text message that came in.
* You check your e-mail several times a day and take precious time out of your day to respond to unimportant e-mails.
* You click on a link in your e-mail and end up surfing the web the whole morning instead of getting done what you had planned.
* You want to catch up on Facebook *really quickly* to see if there are any important messages. Before you realize it, you've spent an hour commenting on silly pictures and posts.

To prevent wasting time, you have to learn to focus on the tasks that are the highest priority. By following the eight steps I'll share with you, you'll stay on track and will accomplish your goals with less effort:

1 **Turn distractions off the night before.** Turn off Twitter, Facebook, Skype, Pinterest, YouTube, e-mails, etc. the night before and don't be tempted to turn them on in the morning. How often did you want to get on any of these sites for only a few minutes and then find yourself still looking around hours later? Do whatever it takes to stay focused. If you do need to get online, wait until AFTER you have done your most important tasks of the day and use a timer. If you must be online, there are websites you can sign up for that will block social media sites for a set period.

2 **Write down your three to four top activities for the next day.** When you start your day already prepared by knowing what the most important activities are for that day, you can hit the ground running as soon as you get to your desk. This will help you to be focused on your outcome for the day. At the top of your list should be your top-income-producing activities.

This is an example of what one of my daily activity lists looks like:

1. Set up new marketing funnel.
2. Schedule five appointments with new clients.
3. Set up auto-responder e-mail to current customers regarding current promotion.
4. Listen to one hour of Eric Lofholm's sales training.
5. Check e-mail, Facebook, YouTube, and Twitter.

You'll notice that the income-producing activities come BEFORE checking Facebook, YouTube, and Twitter. As much as you would love to find out just what your friends are doing today and what coffee they are ordering at Starbucks, you can't allow that silly curiosity to hold you back from reaching your dreams. It's just not worth it! As you check stuff off throughout the day, you'll get a huge feeling of satisfaction and accomplishment.

3 **Take a moment to regroup.** When you are working on many projects, it's easy to become overwhelmed. An easy way to prevent this from happening is to take time to regroup and prepare for your next task. You'll be more clearheaded and

focused. It doesn't take long to regroup, and it can make a world of difference. It helps balance you.

* Close your eyes and take a few deep breaths.
* Get up and look outside the window.
* Step away from your desk.
* Take a break and go for a walk (in nature if possible).

4 **Start tracking your time.** Grab a pen and paper and make a note at the top of each hour of what you have accomplished in the last sixty minutes. This is a great exercise to see what you are actually *doing* with your time—not what you *think* you are doing. This can be a real eye-opener. You'll be shocked by the time you waste!

5 **Set HARD mini deadlines.** Schedule time for each project that you are working on. For example, schedule to write a blog post from 10 to 11 a.m. Work on it during that time frame. Once the deadline hits, you're done. You have what you have. This is a fantastic way to work intensely and with absolute focus for short bursts of time. It is amazing how much you can get done when you create urgency. If you look at the clock and you only have fifteen more minutes left to complete the job, you'll work faster. By mentally setting a specific time to finish something, chances are you'll make it a priority.

6 **Check your e-mail and social media only once per day.** Open it, answer it, close it, and leave it closed! This has increased my available productive hours at least ten-fold.

7 **Every night, document your end of day report.** Make a list of everything you've produced that day, starting with the highest income-producing activities at the top.

✴ How many new clients did you contact?

✴ How many current customers did you follow up with?

✴ Did you learn any new skills today?

✴ How much income did you produce today?

✴ Did you forge any new business connections?

This helps to see in writing what you have done that day—and what you have not done! If you realize that you haven't been productive, then take a good hard look at what you need to do differently, course correct, and measure your improvement. Keep reviewing your results and adjusting your actions!

8 **Hold yourself accountable.** People perform better when they know others are watching them. It is easier to let yourself down than someone who is counting on you. Get an accountability partner or join a Mastermind Group. Everybody thrives with support and encouragement.

My hope is that the strategies in this chapter will help you find more balance in your life. They have taken me from being in tears and feeling utterly inadequate with very little focus, to a life where I have specific steps and strategies to keep me on track and moving forward toward my goals. I am now a successful coach and part

of an incredible community. Let me know how I can help you follow these same steps and get you on your way to completing your goals. Just remember: your daily actions will determine your long-term success. Are you making your time count?

— ABOUT THE AUTHOR —

Sigrid McNab is a successful Internet marketing expert, mentor, and coach. Sigrid's passion is helping entrepreneurs, online marketers, and small business professionals implement those strategies that significantly increase businesses sales, profits, and productivity. She lives in Canada with her husband and two incredible children. She loves horses, all kinds of animals and has a zest for life! Visit her website at www.sigridmcnab.com. Email her at sigrid@sigridmcnab.com. Connect with her on Facebook at http://www.facebook.com/SigridMcNab or please call her on her direct line at 250-954-8416. Let her know how she can help you!

CHAPTER 7

Stepping Into Your Greatness

By Tim Scogin

"What lies behind us and what lies before us are tiny matters compared to what lies within us" – Ralph Waldo Emerson

e have all been fed the story of what our life should be like: we get a college degree, find a stable career, and work the same boring job for forty years before we retire and finally be happy and truly fulfilled. Well, I'm here to tell you that you don't have to settle. You can live your dreams, do what you love, and be successful. There is greatness within all of us that is just begging to be released. I know from personal experience.

After working in the corporate world for twenty-six years, I knew that I was destined for greater things. That morning commute in chaotic traffic was just not doing it for me anymore, not that it ever did. I had a burning desire to be and do more. It was like I knew all along that I wanted something else for my life. So,

I retired when I was offered the chance, and I started living my dream of being my own boss and setting my own hours. You can do the same!

Begin with Personal Development

Just as it did for me, your journey starts with personal development so you can become a better person and live a better, richer life. By gaining knowledge and new skills you can inspire and touch people in a way that gives them the tools to change their situation for the better. Whether you read the Bible for thirty minutes a day, a motivational book like this one, or you take a course, the right knowledge will keep you on track with your goals.

It is an investment into your future and your education, so I don't recommend you to be frugal. And don't just read great books once. Read them twice, three times, or more because each time you read them, you will learn something new. Be sure to highlight and take notes as well.

Below is a list of recommended books:
* *The Bible*
* *Think and Grow Rich* - Napoleon Hill
* *Twelve Pillars* - Jim Rohn and Chris Widener
* *The Charge* - Brendon Burchard
* *The Richest Man Who Ever Lived* - Steven K. Scott
* *The Seasons of Life* - Jim Rohn
* *The Richest Man In Babylon* - George S. Clason

There are many more great books you can choose from. If you want to read the Bible, start with a chapter of Proverbs each day. The point here is that you start reading and learning. Build up your knowledge base, and in the words of the late and great Jim Rohn, "Don't be lazy in language."

In addition to reading, I have used several techniques in changing my life around that I want to share with you. Before using these techniques, I was just following along with the masses. I would get up, go to work, come home, eat, and watch TV until I fell asleep on the couch. The next morning, I would get up and do it all over again. These techniques took me from being lost and floundering with no direction in life to having purpose and goals and to becoming a mentor and an inspiration to others who had lost hope and needed some guidance. Now, I get up with purpose and make a difference in the lives of everyone I come into contact with. I have more confidence than ever before to go out, talk with people, and share my knowledge and experiences with them. These techniques changed my life, and they can change yours.

Say Affirmations Daily

Affirmations are positive declarations that you write down on sticky notes or on paper or print out and frame. You want to put them in a place where you will see them when you get up in the morning and before you go to bed. It really worked for me to gain confidence and manifest abundance.

To start, write down at least ten affirmations.

Here are some examples from my own list:

* I am attracting a wealth of abundance today.
* I am having an amazing day today and I will be an inspiration to all the people I meet.
* I attract success and abundance into my life because this is who I am.
* I meet the right person precisely at the perfect time.
* I am impeccable with my word from this day forward.

Your affirmations should match up to who you are and what it is you want out of life. Sit down and make a list of them, and put them up where you can see them each day: on your bathroom mirror, the fridge, your computer. Say them out loud each morning for fifteen minutes, believing that this is already your reality. You can do this while having your morning coffee, tea, and breakfast. Then, in the evening before you go to bed say your affirmations again for fifteen minutes, so they are fresh in your mind as you fall asleep. This way, they are carried over into your dreamscape!

My list of daily affirmations has helped me to bring things into my life that sometimes not even I can explain. There was a time when I had no money, overdue bills, creditors calling, and too much month at the end of my money. I used the affirmation that "Money flows freely to me every day." Within a couple of days, a check showed up in the mail for just enough money

to pay all my bills and get the creditors to stop calling. My belief in my affirmations was so strong I manifested my desire. Affirmations just go back to the saying, "What you think about, you bring about."

Create a Vision Board

Vision boards, also be known as dream boards, are a visual tool used to keep you focused on your goals and desires, by imprinting images in your mind. This could be anything, from being a speaker, going on vacation to exotic places to having a dog or owning luxury items like a mansion on the beach, a yacht or a nice car. A vision board keeps your vision in front of your eyes.

What are vision boards exactly, and how do you create one? I used a 3'x3' white board with one sticky side; you can find them at a hobby store. Pick up some magazines that have pictures of places you would like to travel to, luxury cars you would like to have, or whatever item you really dream of owning. Then, thumb through those magazines and just tear out what you want. Also cut out words that inspire you. You can cut out a bunch of words and put them together to make an inspiring message. Then take your scissors and cut out every image you want to put on your board.

* Fill the board up with the pictures of places that you want to travel to or that inspire you, words that inspire you, images of the body you would like to have, and more.

✳ Take the images you have cut out and place them over those in a way that they are all converging to the middle (Oasis) of the board.

✳ Arrange words on the board to fit with the pictures; this will give a 3D effect.

Be sure and arrange your images before putting it on the board so that you can see how it will look before actually sticking it down. Once you have completed your vision board, take fifteen minutes each morning and night along with your affirmations to look at it and be motivated to achieve your dreams and goals. As you stare at your vision board say your affirmations and watch as the 3D effect jumps out at you.

Keep a Journal

If you go back through the ages, you will find that journaling has been in practice for many centuries. Many scholars have used journaling as a means to put their thoughts down on paper so that they could go back and reference them later. Keep a journal of the things that inspire you – quotes or people who have touched your life. Write everything down and be sure and date it.

A journal allows you to capture a day in your life that otherwise would be lost to time and lost in thought. You can then refer back to your journal for inspiration and motivation, and when you are speaking or training, you can use your notes to teach.

"Every journey in life is wrought with obstacles and when you have built a solid foundation, those obstacles and those bumps & bruises become less and lesser of a problem. Yes, they will happen, but it is how you handle them that will lead to your success." - Tim Scogin

Take Action

Taking all of these techniques and putting them into action will help you in both your life and business. The key words here are PUT INTO ACTION! If you don't take action, the techniques I shared will just be words on a page. Instill in your mind how you want to look or be and how to get rid of those beliefs that limit your thinking and that cause you to procrastinate and lose sight of your vision.

You must work harder on yourself than you do on your job. Create your vision, work toward it, and create a new life. Remember that successful people don't compete, they create! Just think of the possibilities as you expand your knowledge each day. They are endless! You can do this. All you have to do is decide and TAKE ACTION!

"For things to change...you must change." - Jim Rohn

— ABOUT THE AUTHOR —

Tim Scogin is a certified personal trainer/wellness Coach with TJK Nutrition. After twenty-six years of working for the post office, Tim retired to pursue his dream of teaching others how tapping into their inner energy can help them to manifest their dreams. He is an expert at creating dream/vision boards and using the power of affirmations and the boards to manifest one's dreams. In his spare time, he likes to ride his 2003 Harley Davidson Fatboy, workout, and hike in the mountains. You can contact Tim by phone at (720) 315-0860 or by email at tscogin52@gmail.com.

CHAPTER **8**

Being Open to the Unexpected

By Jacqueline A Kane, Ph.D.

"Opportunity dances with those already on the dance floor."
— H. Jackson Brown

A mother wished to encourage her small girl's interest in the piano, so she took her daughter to a local concert featuring an excellent pianist. As they found their seats near the front of the concert hall, the little girl eyed the Steinway waiting on stage. Soon, the mother found a friend to talk to, and as the women got lost in conversation, the girl quietly slipped away. At eight o'clock sharp, the lights in the auditorium dimmed, the spotlights came on, and only then did the mother notice her daughter sitting at the great piano and quietly picking out the notes of "Twinkle Twinkle Little Star."

The audience's amusement turned to curiosity when the great pianist crossed the stage, walked up to the little girl, and quietly

said, "Keep playing." The pianist sat down beside her, listened for a few seconds, and whispered some words of encouragement. He then began quietly to play a bass accompaniment. A few bars later, he reached around the little girl to add more accompaniments. Together, the old master and the young novice held the crowd mesmerized with their beautiful, blended music. At the end of the impromptu performance, the audience applauded loudly as the pianist took the little girl back to her seat.

We are Not So Different

Like the little girl, we all have goals in our lives—specific things we would like to have or achieve. To do this, we must recognize help when it is offered, just as she did, and we must be open to opportunities to learn great lessons even when it seems like there are none. By being open to opportunities that are presented to us, defining a goal, being aware of obstacles, and persisting, we can achieve those goals. We all have different backgrounds and experiences, yet there is a common thread that I will show you using my own story as a guide.

When I was the director of the Resource Center on Women in Higher Education, I learned the value of being open to opportunities. In the fall of 1976, I attended a conference with a group of affirmative action officers from the State University of New York at the Sagamore Conference Center in the Adirondacks. At the conference, I approached a group of men, all of whom were African American, and I asked them what I could do in my role

as the resource director. Their response was that anything I did should specifically support black women.

When I returned to Albany, New York, I asked my assistant what she thought we could do. She suggested that we sponsor a conference for black women. I had access to an extensive network through my contacts in opportunity programs and with an organization now known as the American Counseling Association, so she and I put together a team of black women from across the state, asking them to become part of the planning committee for the first conference.

Be Prepared to Jump in With Both Feet

When you set goals that involve others, there is a greater chance for fulfillment. Look at the opportunities that exist in your own path, they don't have to be like mine. Ask yourself where is it that you can provide a positive impact on others? How would you go about it? Don't assume you have all the answers, so ask others for their input. Once you have established a goal and a game plan, you need to take action. Many people get to this stage and freeze. You can always find an excuse not to take action, for example, "This is a wrong time" or "I'm not sure what to do."

When I began organizing the conference, I wasn't sure exactly what to do. The team I put together wasn't organized for any specific purpose, and I wasn't quite sure what opportunities would present themselves. However, we were prepared to take appropriate actions in response. I began to see needs and places

where change could be made that would support black women.

With the help of a great planning committee, a conference was held at Manhattanville College in June 1977 with seventy-five attendees. At the close of this conference, the participants decided to take advantage of the gathering and planned to have a second conference soon after. The planning committee convened, and additional members were added from those who attended the Manhattanville Conference. In January 1978, the second conference was held in Albany, New York.

Do Not Allow Your Efforts to Become Stagnant

Just as we set up a second conference right away, you need to determine how to best to keep your game plan going. It's the continuity of action that brings the best results. Along the way pay attention to your results; sometimes a course correction is necessary. You started off with some uncertainty and learned a lot in your pursuit. Take advantage of that new knowledge. Listen to others, get their feedback and reassess your goals often.

After the second successful conference, the planning committee continued to meet. As we convened, a couple of needs became obvious. The first need was simply a chance for black women to get together. These women wanted to have a place to meet and talk about their lives, their goals, and their careers. The committee decided to have an annual conference, and we felt that an official organization was needed to ensure continuity. We decided to call the new organization the Association of Black Women in Higher

Education (ABWHE), and in June 1978, ABWHE held its first conference. Over 200 black women attended.

This conference was simply an opportunity for women to share their research interests and get feedback from other women, allowing them to see different perspectives. We also produced a conference report, allowing the presenters to have additional visibility for their presentations and research. A keynote address series was also created with the intention to provide more diversity and varied subject matter. A quarterly newsletter allowed members to stay in touch and updated between conferences.

Through my activities with ABWHE, I was open to opportunities to both learn and apply what I had learned. In those first few years, I learned how to design and layout the content for all of the ABWHE publications. While coordinating and planning the conference, I learned about recruiting, managing vendors, and managing exhibit space. In promoting the conference, I even learned how to prepare mailings in compliance with U.S. Postal Service requirements. I learned about print media outlets for placing ads and how to use press releases to get publicity. I have used many of the experiences and skills I developed while planning these conferences over and over again in my activities with other organizations and in my various business ventures.

ABWHE still exists today and has grown to be a national organization with chapters that provide numerous opportunities for black women in all aspects of higher education and act to receive and give both support and encouragement.

Every Goal Can Generate a New One

Think of the little girl in the story. After that experience, do you think she stopped playing the piano? Keep an open mind and think out of the box. What have you learned about yourself during this experience? For me, it resulted in considering a career change. What will it mean for you?

There came a point in my life where it was clear that I needed to make a decision about what to do with my career. I began to look around to see what my options were. In doing so, I had to consider some of the obstacles I might encounter when making any kind of career move. I had to ask questions about the possibilities.

Where should I look for my next position? I thought it would be logical to go back on campus to look for opportunities. I enjoyed my relationships with the people I met on campus, and I liked the possibilities of the variety of work I could do. When I looked at the positions available that paid comparably and would allow me to use the skills I had gained from my experience, I found that I couldn't get the right job without a doctorate. So, I decided to go back to school and earn a doctorate.

The next question I had to answer was "What type of degree and what discipline?" I started to do some fact finding. An ABWHE founder told me while I was still on campus, she had observed many candidates for positions at the college were screened out because they had an Ed.D. rather than a Ph.D. Since I hadn't yet decided what direction to take in a career, I felt I needed to give myself as many options as possible, so I chose

to go for a Ph.D. degree. Receiving an Ed.D. could eventually prove to be an obstacle.

I turned to sociology, which was my undergraduate major. I realized that it did not make sense to learn another academic discipline, methodology, and/or terminology. In addition, although not every institution had a sociology department, sociology is taught at any institution that has a liberal arts program. This meant that if it did not work out being an administrator, I would have the option of being able to go to the classroom. The decision about which doctorate to pursue made my goal clear. I also knew what I wanted my research to focus on.

Be Open for the Next Opportunity or Goal

Now that you have found success in the first goal, don't put the blinders on. How can you take advantage of your experiences? Be open for the opportunity to serve others along the way and do not place limits on yourself. Ask questions and do your research. Look inward to find your burning desire. What is it that you would do almost anything to achieve? How can it be used to make a positive impact? Along the way your focus may change. It may require setting different goals. That doesn't mean your original approach was wrong, it means you are learning and are prepared to overcome any obstacle that comes your way.

Through my professional activities, I knew a number of black women in doctoral programs who were having all kinds of challenges getting through their programs. In particular, they

were having difficulties at the dissertation stage where they were not allowed to do research on the topics that they wanted to and had to radically change their topics in order to get support from their department and/or advisors. So as I thought about pursuing a doctoral program, I started asking folks who were in sociology about the program at SUNY at Albany, and I spoke with a couple of the faculty who I had met through various activities. I asked them if they thought there would be support for me to do my research on black women in higher education. In some ways, earning a doctorate was the vehicle for me to answer the question: "Why aren't there more black women college presidents?" I thought it very important to be clear about my goal. I got positive responses from the faculty I spoke with, so I applied, got accepted and began the process that took me seventeen years to complete since I continued to work almost full time.

In 2010, when I went to the conference I helped start, I sat in awe of what ABWHE had become. All the ideas about how to offer support black women in the higher education I had heard were being talked about at that conference. I felt that the organization was in good hands, and black women were positioned to continue to make progress in making the academy their home on all levels. I don't know if I could have envisioned everything ABWHE become, and although I did not personally put it in place, the organization was flexible enough to provide what was needed, yet strong enough to grow and mature into a thirty-five-year-old organization.

In taking advantage of the opportunities presented to me, I was able to lay the groundwork for an organization that has continued to exist and evolve for over thirty-five years. When I was looking for what to do with my career, helping hands taught me lessons and gave me support. Even though I did not go back on campus full time after completing my doctorate, I moved to another position and had a productive, engaging, and interesting career with the New York State Education Department. I now use all these experiences and lessons in my consulting business with colleges and universities and in my coaching practice that helps individuals to achieve their personal and professional goals.

Understand that we rarely know what we will ultimately accomplish or what impact any of our actions might make. However, it's clear that if we aren't open to new opportunities, being open to them anywhere we go, and aren't willing to give and receive help, we will fail. We learn from others and we achieve with support from others. You just need to be open to it to succeed.

— ABOUT THE AUTHOR —

Dr. Jacqueline A. Kane is currently an honorary board member of ABWHE. She is an active member of the Albany, NY Alumnae Chapter of Delta Sigma Theta Sorority, Inc. She is also involved in a peer-to-peer counseling program to help participants be themselves fully and live full lives. Jackie launched Kane Consulting and Coaching to continue assisting institutions that could use her expertise and to assist individuals in their goal setting and problem solving. Visit www.kaneconsultingandcoaching.info to discover what coaching can do for you and to claim your free workbook, "5 Steps to Getting Back on Track."

CHAPTER 9

The Road Map to a Passionate Career

By Aurora Wilson

"Success is calling. Pursue and be persistent to reach your goals." - Aurora Wilson

*a*s I walked down the hallway toward the elevator, I was contemplating my life. For fifteen years, I had been sitting at the same desk and examining claims software systems for an insurance company. I didn't like what I saw going on in management, and in my soul, I knew I had more to offer than being on the computer and reviewing files all day. While driving home that night, I prayed for guidance. The job was providing me the security I needed to provide for my children, but at the same time, I felt I had hit the dead zone in my career. Working my current job for another twenty years until retirement was not what I wanted, so I had to start thinking outside the box. Over the

next weeks, my mind started to open up to new possibilities by considering careers I had never looked at before.

One day, I was sitting in the garden, enjoying the beauty of creation, when I felt that God was talking to me and telling me, "It doesn't matter whether you have experience, you know the right people, and you have your Ph.D. I will guide you if you take the next step." So, I started to read books like *Rich Dad, Poor Dad* and found a mentor in Joyce Meyer. By listening to God and my intuition, little by little, the path was revealed to me. My passion was to travel, so by trusting in God, I moved forward by starting my own travel company.

I'm not alone in this feeling that we are destined for something far greater than monotonous jobs. Do *you* have the innate desire to have something greater? Do you feel you are stuck and are ready for a change? Would you like to follow your passion? The greatest satisfaction in life is knowing your purpose and living your passion. You *can* achieve your dreams if you believe and apply the following principles and lessons:

1. **Invest in yourself.** To achieve higher levels of success, you have to be willing to learn and grow. You have to educate yourself about the industry you want to be in and invest in yourself by taking downtime. Make sure that you can function optimally and be focused. Invest in your relationship with God by spending time in prayer and meditation, which will help you to grow strong spiritually, emotionally, and mentally. You need a strong faith system. You need to believe in yourself in order to

have clients believe in you. Speak positive affirmations about your life. When you invest to make yourself a better person, you will attract people who are part of your divine connection circle, and opportunities will come your way.

2   **Identify the need.** Own your expertise. Pick a niche in your industry that will build on your core values. Don't be an imitator. Be an innovator! Research the market, identify a need, and fill it! Make sure that you are passionate about what you are doing because that will ensure that you won't give up. For me, when the economy went down after 9/11, the travel industry took a hit, and I had to find another source of income. I loved health care and enjoyed helping people. As a teenager, I used to help two seniors who lived in my neighborhood. I also helped my grandmother understand her insurance needs and assisted her with her medical appointments. Having worked in the healthcare industry, I had seen many patients who were misinformed about their medical care options, medical insurance, claims, and medical bills.

When I was fighting cancer and feeling terribly sick, it was frustrating that the doctor didn't want to listen to my needs. He told me only what his textbook said. I then had to convince every medical provider that I knew my rights because each one tried to take advantage of me. On top of that, many surgical procedures required that I had somebody pick me up and stay with me for twenty-four to forty-eight hours. They didn't let me take a cab, and they didn't allow

me to drive myself either. Well, I had just moved to a new city and didn't know anyone I could ask. It took me several days of calling to finally find a company that could help me because most companies cater to long-term care or seniors.

From this painful experience, I identified the gap my skills and experience could fill, and I started a company to help consumers become better informed about their health care options and to help those who are dealing with a medical issue navigate the healthcare system.

3 Be willing to make sacrifices. In order to achieve success, you will have to make sacrifices along the way. Success requires motivation, dedication, persistence, and patience. When I started my own business, I didn't know where my next client would come from. I sacrificed a social life and lots of sleep because I was studying and working hard day and night, and I had to give up the stable income I was used to having as a manager in corporate America. Keep in mind that a temporary sacrifice today will result in fulfillment tomorrow if you are living your God-given calling.

The biggest sacrifice was when my eighteen-year-old son was murdered in 2013. It was the hardest time of my life. I was devastated, but I continued to focus on what I could offer others and didn't allow myself to get caught up in pity or depression. Lots of prayer and having strong spiritual women around me helped me to keep moving forward. I truly believe that there are greater rewards from God when you give to others unselfishly.

It taught me that life truly is too short, and tomorrow is not a promise. We must live in fullness every day.

4 **Know your true worth.** Your true worth is immeasurable and extremely expansive! You have the power to achieve the desired results you envision for your life regardless of your background or where you are today. Once you learn to recognize your self-worth, you'll be able to see what you have to offer to the world and what God has called you to be. Instead of allowing your experiences to make you feel inadequate, utilize them to create the life you want to live. Design your path while you enjoy the journey along the way.

I grew up with a self-defeated attitude and no self-worth, believing what others said about me because I was abused and bullied. Living in a low-income neighborhood and not having much, I believed the people around me who said I wouldn't amount to anything. At twenty-one years old, I was a single mom of three boys, wanting more for my life and for my sons. Studying the Bible and reading self-help books allowed me to heal within and stop believing the lies I had been told all my life. Learn to trust and believe in yourself. You are your greatest fan and supporter!

5 **Create a road map.** Establishing a career you are passionate about is very fulfilling. Being able to help others by doing what you love will be much more rewarding than just letting your life pass away as you work for a pay check.

These steps will help you in the process:

✻ Find your purpose and calling.

✻ Identify your personal values.

✻ Write a clear personal vision statement.

✻ Develop a strategy plan.

✻ Believe in yourself, but don't take on more than you can handle.

✻ Be dedicated to your success.

✻ Find a niche that combines your passion, talents, skills and experience.

My life's journey has not been easy. Having suffered abandonment, abuse, domestic violence, hunger, and homelessness, I worked hard to survive and defy the odds. Despite my childhood hardships, the major financial loss from my business in 2008, my two-year battle with cervical cancer, my fight with auto-immune disease, and the death of loved ones, I didn't become a victim of my life experiences. Instead, I became a victor. What got me through and helped me to stand steadfast through an avalanche of adversity wasn't the size of my bank account, but it was the power of my vision, my faith in God, and my dreams. You have to live by faith and not by sight. You will be tested, and you may feel frightened, but be patient and take your time. Success will happen! Pursue your dreams and be persistent. You will achieve your goals. Live your brilliant life!

— ABOUT THE AUTHOR —

Aurora Wilson is the founder of Aurora Health Care Advocacy. Her company guides clients through the forest of the healthcare system by educating individuals about their rights and options, providing patients with practical help and giving them the information they need regarding Medicaid, Medicare, coding, billing, claims, etc. Aurora is a member of the National Healthcare Advocacy Organization. She is also a licensed and ordained minister, a certified life coach, and a member of the International Coaching Federation. Her books *The Awakening Moment* and *My Journey Home* will be released Summer 2014. You can reach Aurora at 770-8-AURORA (828-7672) or via email aurora@aurorawilson.com. www.aurorawilson.com and www.aurorahealthcareadvocacy.com

CHAPTER 10

The Ten-Step Goal-Setting Process to Create the Life of Your Dreams

By Eric Lofholm

> *"Though no one can go back and make a brand new start,*
> *anyone can start from now and make a brand new ending."*
> *- Carl Bard*

*T*he speaker asked, "How many of you consider yourselves goal setters?" Probably 99% of the attendees at this personal development seminar raised their hands. He then said, "Let's find out. Take out a clean sheet of paper. Write down ten goals. You have three minutes. Go."

Just like everyone else, I began to write. At the end of the three minutes, I only had seven goals written down. I was surprised that I wasn't able to come up with ten. The speaker then asked the group, "How many of you were able to come up with ten goals?" About fifty hands went up, even though there were over one thousand

people in the room. Only 5% were able to complete this simple exercise. He explained that the reason most of us were unable to complete the exercise is that we weren't goal setters. He said, "For a goal to be a goal, it must be written down. Most people think that goal setting is merely deciding what you want. That's only the first step. Goal setting is a process. If you are not following the process, then what you are doing is not goal setting." He taught us his process, and I was fascinated. All along I thought I had been goal setting, but in that moment, I realized that I had not.

After that day, I continued to study goal setting. I collected the most powerful and successful principles in the world and used them to create my own ten-step goal setting process that can teach anyone quickly and easily how to create the life of his or her dreams. To understand the goal setting process, however, you should know some basics.

Why should I set goals and write them down?

Setting goals is one of the most misunderstood personal development ideas. Many people believe they are goal setters just like I did back then, yet they fail to write down their goals—the one strategy consistently used by the most successful people in the world. So why doesn't everyone use goal setting as a strategy to realize their dreams? I've found that there are several specific reasons why people do not set goals:

1. They don't know the importance of goal setting.
2. They don't know how.

3. They think they are already doing it.

4. They don't have any goals.

5. They are afraid of failure.

6. They don't believe in themselves.

7. They suffer from the curse of early success.

8. They are in a comfort zone.

9. They are afraid of success.

But you can't let those reasons stop you from setting and writing down goals and ultimately achieving those goals. There are clear benefits of goal setting that you will not get from any other strategy:

1. Written goals help reduce stress by creating a compelling future for you.

2. Written goals guide you to move in the right direction.

3. Written goals activate your subconscious mind.

4. Written goals help you clearly communicate your life plans to others.

5. Written goals increase the likelihood that you will achieve your goals by 100%.

6. Written goals clarify how to invest your time.

7. Written goals motivate you.

8. Written goals help you attract what you want.

9. Written goals help you create the life of your dreams.

The Ten-Step Goal-Setting Process

When I designed this process, I wanted to combine the most effective goal-setting strategies with the easiest application. While I was creating this system, many of the processes I looked at were either too complicated or didn't give enough information to be effective. The following system is designed with you in mind. If you follow these ten simple steps in order, you can turn your dreams into reality.

1. **Think about what you want and write it down.** What is your dream? Where do you want to travel? How much money do you want to have when you retire? What is your ideal job? The goal-setting process starts with thinking about what you want and how you want your life to be. One simple way to get started is by asking questions.

   I wanted to lose weight. I had low energy and poor eating habits. During my brainstorming session, I asked myself several health-related questions like, "How do I want to feel when I wake up in the morning? What would my ideal weight be? What type of foods do I want to put into my body? What foods should I be avoiding?" My answers became my thought menu: "I want to feel energized when I wake up in the morning. My ideal body weight is 185 pounds. I want to eat more fruits and vegetables. I should avoid fast food, ice cream, and soda."

2. **Decide exactly what you want and write it down.** The second step in goal-setting is to decide exactly what you want.

Be as specific as you can. For example, write down "I want to earn $100,000 over the next twelve months" instead of "I want to make more money next year." The second sentence would not be specific enough. For my weight loss goal, if I had said, "I want to lose weight and eat better," that wouldn't be specific enough.

I had to pinpoint exactly what I wanted. From my thought menu for my weight loss goal, I took one idea to its completion. I decided the specific goal I wanted to achieve was to weigh 185 pounds. I weighed 238, so my goal was to lose 53 pounds.

3 **Make sure your goal is measurable.** Once you have written down your goal, make sure it is measurable so you can know if when you've accomplished your goal. My goal was to weigh 185 pounds. This was a measurable goal, so it passed the test. If your goal isn't measurable, go back to Step 2 and rewrite your goal, making sure that it's measurable.

4 **Identify the specific reasons you want this goal and write them down.** Most people fail to achieve their goals because they don't have a compelling enough reason to achieve them. Once you have begun the ten-step goal-setting process, you are ready to take action. Along the path toward achieving your goals, you will run into some obstacles. That is where your *why* comes in. If your reason for achieving the goal is greater than the obstacles you face, then you will be much more likely to achieve the goal. If you don't have a strong

enough reason, then imagine one. Spend some time really thinking about what it would mean to you to accomplish the goal. Also think about what the consequences would be if you didn't accomplish the goal.

Let's say you've been smoking a pack of cigarettes per day for eighteen years. You've had a goal to quit smoking for the last six years because you know smoking isn't good for you. You followed proper goal-setting techniques. You tried gum, hypnosis, and quit-smoking seminars. Nothing seemed to work. You go to the doctor, and the doctor says you have lung cancer. If you quit smoking now, you will have ten years to live. If you keep smoking, you will die in one year. Would you be able to quit smoking? I think you (and most people) would. Even though it was a goal of yours for the last six years and you weren't able to succeed, I believe you would be able to quit now. You would have a strong enough reason to accomplish the goal.

Write a paragraph about why you must succeed in achieving your goal. Once you have completed the paragraph, read it over. Then ask yourself the question, "Do I have a big enough *why* to overcome the obstacles I'm going to encounter?"

This was the *why* to my weight loss: "I must lose fifty-three pounds because this is not the person I really am. I am sick and tired of people thinking of me as fat. I want to run a marathon before I die, and I will never be able to do it at this weight." I then looked at my paragraph. I believed I

had a strong enough reason to overcome the obstacles I was going to face, so I continued with the process. If your *why* isn't compelling enough, go back and rewrite it.

5 Establish a definite date for accomplishment of your goal and write it down. It is very important to decide when you want to accomplish your goal. Your mind has an unconscious timeline, and it needs to start working on plans for how you will make your goal happen. Knowing when you want to accomplish your goal will also have an effect on how you plan to achieve it. For example, the goal of earning $100,000 in the next twelve months is very different from having a goal of earning $100,000 any time in the future. Once you write down an end date for your goal, your mind will start working toward achieving it.

The only way to take advantage of your mind is to set a date and enter it into your subconscious by writing it down. For my weight loss goal, I gave myself a timeline of six months.

6 List the action steps you need to take to accomplish your goal and write them down. Ask yourself, "What are the steps I need to take to accomplish my goal?" This is a brainstorming exercise. Here we are looking to capture as many ideas as possible—we call this the action steps menu. Once again, we want as many choices as possible to create our plan, and we aren't looking for the steps to be in order at this point. Take out a clean sheet of paper and write anything and everything

that comes to mind—things you will need to do in order to achieve your goal. These were my action steps menu for my weight loss goal:

* Go to the health food store to get good food.

* Exercise three times per week.

* Take a multi-vitamin every day.

* Meet with a nutrition expert to establish a diet.

* Meet with an exercise specialist to create a workout program.

* Create a tracking system to track my results.

* Buy an exercise book.

* Talk to my friend Bob (Bob lost 30 pounds last year) to find out how he lost weight.

Notice that the list isn't in any particular order. Once you have listed as many ideas as you can, go to the next step.

7 **Create an action plan from your list of action steps and write it down.** Step 7 is where your thoughts mesh into a plan. To create your plan, take your action steps from above and put them into sequential order, prioritizing them. Don't let the word *plan* scare you. This is a simple exercise.

1. Talk to my friend Bob (Bob lost 30 pounds last year) and find out how he lost weight.

2. Buy an exercise book.

3. Make an appointment to meet with a nutrition expert to establish a diet.

4. Make an appointment to meet with an exercise specialist to create a workout plan.
5. Meet with the nutrition expert.
6. Go to the health food store to get good food.
7. Take a multi-vitamin every day.
8. Meet with the exercise specialist.
9. Create a tracking system to track my results.
10. Exercise three times per week.

Most people think creating an action plan is a lengthy process, and the word "plan" becomes intimidating. However, my plan only took a few minutes of thought. When you create a plan to achieve a goal, ask yourself, "If I follow the plan, will I achieve the goal?" For my weight-loss goal, I thought, "If I execute the plan, can I lose 53 pounds in six months?" The answer was yes!

 Take action. Every step in the ten-step goal-setting process is important, and each step depends upon the others. This step, however, could be the most important. I can't tell you how many educated derelicts I have met over the years—you know, the people who know everything about everything, yet can't seem to get themselves to take action in their own lives. Goals and plans are great, but they don't produce results.

Action is the only thing that produces results. How many times have you planned to do something, yet when it came to the action phase, you didn't act? Start on your goal right away, even if it's small act. In my weight-loss example, one small action I

took right away was to go to the health food store and pick out some food. That was a positive step toward the achievement of my goal. It was a small step, but it helped me create momentum. Another step I took was to jog for two minutes the first day. That might not seem like a lot, but it really was. Most people never achieve their goals because they never take the first step. They never benefit from the law of momentum: a body in motion tends to stay in motion. Remember, the journey of a thousand miles begins with just one step. Many people try too much too soon and get overwhelmed. If you try to make your goal happen instantly, you're more likely to get discouraged and quit. Inch by inch, it's a cinch.

Do something every day. Work toward the achievement of your goals every day, even if you only take a small step. Remember: inch by inch, it's a cinch. When you take action on a consistent basis, even if it is a small step, you take advantage of the law of momentum and the motion you start with your first step. Rome wasn't built in a day, and your major life goals aren't going to happen overnight in most cases, so practice patience. For instance, for my goal, I decided, "Today, I will make an appointment with Bob to find out how he was able to lose weight." This action is still just a tiny step toward the achievement of my goal, yet it will keep the momentum going. By taking this small step, I used the law of momentum in my favor. To keep momentum going, write down the positive steps you take toward your goal.

10 **View your goals as often as possible.** Out of sight, out of mind—human beings don't have the best memories. You have already invested the time to complete steps one through nine. Now that your goals are written down with a plan, you can quickly review five to ten goals in a matter of minutes. The more frequently you view your goals, the more you will burn them into your subconscious mind. Something magical happens when you do that. After some time of frequently reviewing your goals and their plans of action, your subconscious mind will believe you are going to achieve them. Once you have accomplished that, you can take advantage of the most powerful personal development idea ever discovered: our thinking becomes reality!

Notice, with the exception of Step 8 (take action), every step requires that you think about what you want. Since our thinking becomes reality, we become what we think about. This is one of the secrets of this ten-step process. It requires that you invest time thinking about what you want most in your life. Many people who do not achieve their goals invest their time in thinking of all the reasons they can never succeed in their lives, or they invest their time thinking of ways to solve other people's problems. They may even invest their time in thinking about the fact that they have no money. There is nothing wrong with thinking about these things. However, if you choose to invest your time thinking this way, just realize the consequences. Our thinking becomes reality.

My Challenge to You

You have just learned the most powerful goal-setting process in the world. I challenge you to take action, to implement these proven principles, and to create the life of your dreams. I challenge you right now to take advantage of the law of momentum and take the first step in the goal-setting process to find the success you deserve.

— ABOUT THE AUTHOR —

Eric Lofholm is a Master Sales Trainer who has trained tens of thousands of sales professionals nationwide. His clients have added millions of dollars to their sales bottom line after attending Eric's energetic and groundbreaking seminars. Ever since the beginning of his career in sales, he has maintained a track record of outperforming his fellow sales reps. He has been trained by top trainers like Anthony Robbins and Donald Moine, Ph.D. Many of America's top companies hire Eric regularly to train, motivate, and inspire their sales teams. www.saleschampion.com.

CHAPTER 11

Attracting Clients From the Inside Out

By Stephanie Donegan

"A person is limited only by the thoughts that he chooses."
- James Allen

*L*aura and Susan are sisters whose parents owned a small mom-and-pop travel agency. The business was doing OK —not a huge success, but far from a failure. They both worked in the family business and their parents stressed the importance of owning your own business.

As they grew up they each followed their own path, Laura decided against going to a major university; instead, she went to a two-year community college, and started her own accounting business with less than $100. Even though her only work experience had been working for her parents, she had big dreams of clients who loved her work and loved paying her for her services. Laura

had good memories of her youth. She remembered how happy her parents were. They always had smiles on their faces, enjoyed spending time with family, and working in the business, even though they didn't have a lot of money. She wanted to follow their model: Enjoying the work you do and being happy.

Susan spent four years at UCLA, went to law school and became an attorney. Immediately after finishing law school, Susan's goal was to build one of the most successful firms in Los Angeles and she opened her own firm. Thinking back on her childhood she remembered how her parents were struggling — and she hated it. It was something that she wanted to get as far away from as possible. They couldn't afford to travel and to the things they wanted.

At first glance, the cards seemed stacked against Laura. She didn't have much experience outside of her parents business, and she only had a two year degree. Yet within a year, Laura began to see amazing levels of success. Laura's goal was to create a freedom-based business that she could run from anywhere in the world. A week in Paris, two weeks in Dubai—she was doing it all, all while having clients pay her royally for her services. There wasn't much of a difference between what Laura did and what any other business accountant did, yet clients flocked to her and never questioned her high-end price tags.

Susan's business didn't kick off so well for her. The more she tried, pushed, struggled, and hustled, the harder it seemed. She felt like she was destined to live the same life as her parents—one of struggle.

When I met these ladies at a conference in 2012 I was extremely interested to hear their stories. At this point, Laura's company was well over the six-figure mark, and she was truly living her dreams. Susan on the other hand was still in a place of unhappiness and struggle.

Where are you in life? Does your business look like Laura's company where you get paid very well for what you love to do? Or can you relate more with Susan? Do you feel that no matter how hard you work you are not getting anywhere? What was the difference between the two sisters? After all, they had the same parents, the same upbringing and the same entrepreneurial foundation. Laura was looking at the glass half-full, while Susan was looking at the glass half-empty. Both women set goals for their lives and their business, but they came from two different perspectives.

Susan was so busy focusing on the life she *didn't* desire that she didn't allow space to create the life that she *did* desire. It took her months of replacing old belief systems and learn how to focus on how wonderful entrepreneurship is and how easy making money is. We made a plan to create her ideal business. Susan's firm now brings in over $3 million per year, and she is happier than ever. As soon as Susan started focusing on the joys of entrepreneurship, everything changed!

It Starts With You

As a client magnet specialist, clients come to me to help them attract their ideal clients. They come expecting a plethora of tips, tools, techniques, and a logical strategy to reach their ideal clients, but they are often shocked when they realize that they also have to do internal work. Attracting your ideal client starts from the inside out.

Have you ever been on a long trip with several layovers? You'd much rather jump on one plane and go straight to your destination, right? In business, if you are dealing with old belief systems that hold you back, with negative thoughts and feeling surrounding business, and with a pessimistic outlook on life, you are adding layovers to your trip, which could be as simple as jumping on one plane and being there in no time if you have the right outlook.

My life's purpose is to make your trip to your destination as short as possible with no layovers—while flying first class. In order to do that you need to get rid of the gunk and junk that has held you back that often camouflages itself as anxiety, worry, procrastination, visibility issues, doubt, fear, etc. Without dealing with the internal work first, you become an instant client repellant! Once those underlying beliefs are replaced, you can move on to the tools and techniques that attract your client.

"How do you destroy belief systems?" I was raised knowing that I could accomplish anything that I desired. I believed that; and for the first few years of my adult life, it seemed as though everything I touched turned to gold.

I was considered a "lucky person." You know, one of those people who'd leave home with a resume and smile and come home with a dream job for which I wasn't even qualified while everyone else was having trouble getting a job. But after college I got friends from work who were everything but positive. Shortly after changing my environment, my view on life began to change. I heard my new friends say things like, "Never plan because when you do, the plan never works out," and "What can go wrong will," and "Don't count your chickens before they hatch." These all were statements that never were true for me previously, but all of a sudden whatever could go wrong for me did.

See, the belief systems that I picked up were not actually *my* beliefs. They were beliefs of the people that I had allowed into my energy field. That's how most of us are. Our beliefs are actually not our own, but those that we have heard from friends, parents, grandparents, teachers, etc. To rid ourselves of those beliefs, we simply must adopt new ones that correspond with what we want to believe.

To replace the thought "What can go wrong, will," I began to say, "Everything works out perfectly for me." Of course at first I began to feel like a complete liar. At first glance, the thought that I was attempting to wash away seemed to be the true thought, but I kept at it. Every day I'd affirm that everything works out perfectly for me. Soon, everything began to work just like it was supposed to work out.

In order to wash away your current belief systems, you must replace them. Start today. Write down the negative beliefs you have

about accomplishing your goals in business and attracting your ideal clients, then create new belief systems and start affirming them daily. After a short while, you will find that these new beliefs that you are affirming really have become your beliefs. Once your replace your old beliefs, you are only a few steps away from becoming a client magnet and reaching your goals.

The Client Magnet Action Plan:

1 **Get vision.** The first step is to get *vision*. Having vision is the process of seeing the things that you want—not just thinking them, but actually *seeing* them. See your business as you'd like it to be. What does your business look like when it's prosperous? How many clients or customers do you need on a monthly basis to reach your dream financial figure? How many employees do you have? Ensure that your visions surrounding your business and entrepreneurship are positive ones. Having vision is the process of seeing your business the way you'd like it to be ideally. After all, if you don't know what you want in business, how will you create it?

2 **Become visible.** The next step in reaching your goals in business and becoming a client magnet is *visibility*. Once you create and maintain positive thoughts about business, money, entrepreneurship, and any other areas, you will begin to feel comfortable being visible. Think of it like this: if no one knows who you are and what you do, how will you draw them to you? Shout from the rooftops what you do and how

you do it! Hold teleseminars and webinars, speak at events, host Google hangouts and live streams, or even write a book! Get your message in front of as many people as possible. Remember, you were created to serve, and you can't serve if you aren't seen. I have a saying "If you aren't seen, you aren't considered." In order to be a client magnet, our clients have to be able to consider us.

3 **Stay focused.** *Focus* is an important step in attaining goals. As entrepreneurs, we are naturally creative. That means that we are constantly creating and thinking of new things that we can do—the next big thing. You have to make a conscious decision to focus on one thing and allow it to grow. When you suffer from "shiny object syndrome", you accomplish nothing because you can't focus long enough to create success with any one thing.

If your prospective client sees you on social media today posting about your current business and a totally different business next week, you will cause confusion. Not only will they not know what you stand for, but you also won't be taken seriously. You won't be considered when they think of the "expert" that they need in your field.

I've been there. When I first started out in business, I was all over the place. I didn't even realize it until a friend of mine told me that she didn't really even know exactly what I did! She knew I was an entrepreneur, a natural hair and skin guru, a business coach, a life coach, and some other things she spouted out. I became confused just *listening* to her! I realized that though I thought I was just expressing all the things that I'm passionate about, I was actually confusing my prospective client.

 Create a brilliance box. A Brilliance Box can be a literal box or simply a folder you create on your desktop. It holds all the brilliant ideas that you come up with on a regular basis— the ones you just *know* are money-making ideas that you'd like to pursue. Once your current business is up, running, and able to survive on its own without your attention, you can pick one of your brilliant ideas to then start working on.

Doing this allows you to capture all your great ideas. It may relieve the need to get the idea out, knowing that you can come back to it later, yet you aren't taking time away from your current business that needs your undivided attention at the moment. See, businesses are like children; they go through stages. In the infancy, toddler, and adolescent phase, your business needs lot of attention. Once it gets into the "teen" phase, it can handle a little more independence and freedom. So save those brilliant ideas in the Brilliance Box for the teen phase.

 Be consistent. The last step—and one that goes hand-in-hand with focus—is *consistency*. You must remain consistent— consistent with your branding, your marketing messages, and your visibility. This is extremely important! Don't think that you are going to sell a product or service consistently if your ideal clients and customers don't see you consistently.

Creating goals and reaching them isn't hard. It is as easy as making pasta if you have the recipe. That's why I've created an amazing free training as my gift to you: My proven system showcases the three cornerstones to becoming a client magnet and reach your business goals Faster than ever:

1. Learn to attract clients from the inside out.
2. Put out information that speaks to your ideal client on an emotional level.
3. Take inspired action with your end goal in mind

In order to achieve success in business and attract your ideal clients, you must not only have the tools and the techniques, you need the right mindset to accomplish your goals. Imagine running a wildly successful business that doesn't feel like work at all. Imagine waking up when you want to, home schooling your kids (if you want to), living in the home you desire, traveling the world and all of this working as little as possible. Imagine running an amazingly successful business from your laptop from unbelievable locations. That's pretty hot huh? Well, that's the life that I teach entrepreneurs how to live every day! When it comes to helping business owners turn their businesses that look more like jobs into businesses that provide freedom, I am your go–to girl. For more information please contact me at: http://stephaniedonegan.com/how-to-attract-high-paying-clients/

— ABOUT THE AUTHOR —

Stephanie Donegan has ten years of experience in sales and marketing, helping major Fortune 500 telecommunications companies get their message and their brand out to the masses. She has been featured on NBC, CBS and Fox Business just to name a few. Since branching off in 2009 as a private marketing coach, Stephanie has worked with clients in industries from real estate to health & wellness, telecommunications, tech start-ups and fashion brands. Her clients have gone from little to no revenue to living lives that they only dreamed of within 12 to 18 months by learning to effectively market to their ideal clients and leverage the power of the internet. www.StephanieDonegan.com

CHAPTER 12

Prevent Crashing on Your Chosen Path

By Gerry Werner

> *"To err is human – and to blame it on a computer is even more so." – Robert Orben*

There was one mortgage company that had their own server. The higher-ups knew it was getting old, but they wanted to postpone buying a new one as long as they could. One Friday, their server crashed with all their data on it. I was called in to restore their data from their backups, but the backups were corrupted. In the end, they had to spend thousands of dollars to restore the backups. However, the worst part was that the servers were down for three days—a devastating consequence. Employees could not access their emails or data. The only way to communicate with their clients was by phone, but they could not access the company's database to get those phone numbers. They had to rely on

their clients to call. They didn't even know what had to be done that day. Clients were very angry and upset.

You can imagine the repercussions. In business, it's critical that everything happens in a timely manner, and with this one event, nothing was getting done. The company had been working on million dollar deals, and the realtors and banks they used to work with were not happy with the damage the company had caused, to say to the least.

Think about it: the founder had worked so hard to realize his goal of having his own company. He had spent years building relationships and trust with realtors and banks, and the minute the server went down, so did the reputation that he had diligently built for years.

Technology has become a large part of the way that we achieve our vision. Most people are looking to maximize their productivity and efficiency. This has become easier as the tools have been developed for companies and people to use to speed up their activities. Being efficient and effective in using these tools, specifically tools in information technology, is beneficial in the overall achievement of our vision. Most technologies being used in companies now are larger in scale or are ones that individuals would not normally rely on. It is the goal of my company, GW Technology Solutions, to ensure that whether you are an individual or a business, you are operating at the maximum level of productivity. In order to operate at maximum efficiency, you need to ensure that certain systems are in place. Depending on your focus, you may need physical

devices like computers, laptops, printers, scanners, smartphones, tablets, telephone systems, and other physical technology systems. You will likely also need software systems that provide a way to compose emails and electronic communications, back up your data, and allow you to create various documents to record systems, processes, communications, financial data, and other information. All of these tools help you to set and achieve the goals that you want for your business and yourself while maintaining maximum efficiency. To be effective in your business with these technologies, here are a few tips:

1. Think proactively, not just reactively. Being prepared for disastrous situations will limit the amount of time that is spent correcting the problem.

2. Look at the environment you are working in and understand what needs to be accomplished. Understanding your environment and the result that you need to achieve will increase your preparedness for situations that may arise.

3. Have a solid working knowledge of the technology that you use so that you won't be manipulated.

4. Protect yourself from attackers. Threats to the productive processes of an individual or group will create situations that will stop production or wipe out work you have completed.

5. Remain calm. This will help others feel more confident. One cannot think clearly in a state of panic.

Think Proactively

An attorney I worked with was creating a document, and after meeting with the client, he realized that much of the work he had completed while creating the document needed to be changed. Recreating the document would have been out of the question, as it would have taken him several hours that he did not want to bill to the client but also did not want to lose. As you may know, attorneys are very conscious of time because they bill their clients according to the time it will take to complete the work. Without maximizing their efficiency, they spend more time than they should on a particular task and are not able to bill as much because they do not have as much time to focus on other clients. In order to ensure they are able to help more clients it is very important that their computers and other technology systems operate in a way that provides maximum productivity.

To assist with his dilemma, this attorney contacted me. He knew that I had set backup systems in place to aid in such a situation. Because these systems were in place, we were able to restore an earlier version of the document that he had to make only a few modifications to.

Anticipating these sorts of problems is part of planning. My vision for this law firm was to keep computer system disruptions to a minimum in order to keep the attorneys operating at maximum efficiency. That way, they could gain the most profit from the time they had available. In order for this vision to become a reality, it was necessary to plan for contingencies such as this. In the vision

and goals you set for yourself, make sure that you not only plan for the times when everything will be going well, but also for the times when something may affect your production. Being proactive in your goal setting and planning will allow you to know what needs to be done in those situations to quickly correct the situation or prevent the loss of important data. It can save your hours or even years of work.

Understand Your Environment and What Needs To Be Accomplished

Your vision does not have to be something large scale or long term in order for you to apply the techniques mentioned in this book. It just needs to be something that helps you achieve the goals or meet the needs you have in your environment. For example, I was contacted by a mental health professional's office to assist them in an existing situation that concerned them. One of the systems they had was not working the way that it should. They wanted a form that had been filled out on an iPad to be sent to an assistant who could then work with the information. However, for some reason, this system was not working as they wanted it to, and they were not sure what was causing the problem. After consulting with another technician, they were not optimistic that their problem could be corrected without redeveloping their business process and paying someone to recreate the digital forms that they were using. After some research into the matter, I found the true cause of the problem and made the correction so that it

would work exactly as intended without interrupting any of the existing business processes. The client was very pleased that their process worked as they envisioned it. They didn't need a large-scale system or a major technology change. Instead, they needed a simple addition that made it possible to accomplish their vision.

Have a Working Knowledge of Your Technology and Protect Yourself from Attackers

Having the tools to accomplish your goals is not the same as knowing how to use those tools to attain your vision. Even though we may all have computers, not everyone knows how to use the programs on their computers to accomplish what they want. Not everyone knows how to utilize all the features available to them in Microsoft Outlook or Word. Not everyone knows about the tools that are built into the Windows and Macintosh operating systems.

A solid working knowledge of the technology tools that you are using is immensely beneficial. The benefits can be seen not just in your efficiency, but also in how it keeps you from becoming a victim of manipulation and attacks by others who know the technologies better than you. I had a client who received an email from a questionable source and clicked a link in the email. By doing this, he installed a virus on the computer. Does this sound familiar? He was not aware that the virus protection that he had installed needed to be upgraded to maintain the most current virus definitions, meaning that his virus protection could not help in this situation.

To correct this problem, he contacted a technician who offered to help, but the technician used information about the client's computer to confuse my client and increase the cost of the service that the technician would provide. There was no reason for my client to be concerned about the information that the technician provided him, but because of his lack of knowledge, he was effectively being manipulated into paying money for unnecessary services. Fortunately, he was very smart and saw what was happening. He contacted me, and after evaluating the situation, I was able to explain the actual state of his computer and put him at ease. I knew the client would also be more careful and knowledgeable about potential viruses and attackers in the future.

Remain Calm

You should remain calm when disastrous situations occur. Staying calm helps others who may be panicking feel confident as well. On one occasion, I was helping a bookkeeper with a document she had somehow deleted. This document had been requested by the CEO and had taken a while for her to create. She began panicking before she explained the situation to me. The importance of the retrieval of this document became clear very quickly, so I calmly and confidently stated that "we" would get the document back very quickly so that she could get it to the CEO without him even noticing that anything had gone wrong. Not only did she appreciate the fact that I was able to retrieve the document for her using one of the backup systems I had set in place, but she

also appreciated the fact that I was able to bring her back from the panicked state that she had been stuck in.

A vision, a plan, and effective strategies to increase productivity and minimize downtime will make your technological systems work *for* you rather than against you—no matter what the situation. Not only will you appreciate how prepared you are for the unknown, but the people who you are helping will appreciate this as well. In this increasingly technological world, we must remain up-to-date on new technologies and leverage all the tools available to achieve the vision we have worked so hard to achieve. Don't let a lack of knowledge or the fear of the unknown stop you from succeeding.

"The first rule of any technology used in a business is that automation applied to an efficient operation will magnify the efficiency. The second is that automation applied to an inefficient operation will magnify the inefficiency." - Bill Gates

— ABOUT THE AUTHOR —

With a background in communications, information technology, and business, Gerry Werner has a well-rounded knowledge base and has spent many years working in the information technology field. Gerry has a master's degree in business administration, which has provided him a sound understanding of business, in addition to his bachelor's degrees in interpersonal communication and information technology. He uses those skills in his computer services business, GW Technology Solutions, to benefit others. Whether it is to teach someone to use their iPad, to work on multiple computers and servers, or to solve a problem remotely, Gerry Werner has the experience and ability to help people when they need someone they can count on. Visit www.gwtechsolutions.com or contact Gerry via email at gerry@gwtechsolutions.com or call him at 727-231-1152

CHAPTER 13

Roadmap to Your Success: A Measureable Plan

By Susan Raisanen

"It is a capital mistake to theorize before one has data." -
Sherlock Holmes

*M*aybe you've heard the saying, "A goal is a dream with a deadline." What is the difference between a dream and a goal? Webster's dictionary defines a dream as: *to contemplate the possibility of doing something.* It defines goal as: *the object of a person's ambition or effort; an aim or desired result.* As a business owner, are you just dreaming? Are you just contemplating the possibility of doing or achieving something, or are you actually taking steps to achieve your goals?

Many people don't achieve their goals because they don't know why they selected the goals in the first place. Once you know *why* you want something so badly, then and only then can you get

started with a plan to reach your goal. There must be a strong enough reason if you expect to succeed. Why do you want what you want? Why is the end result of your ambition or desire so important to you?

Once you find your reason, it is time for a road map—an organized plan to reach your goals and the milestone measurements that are along the way and a way to measure and keep you on track. Think back to your elementary school days. Starting in kindergarten or first grade, most students received a folder or a notebook of some sort to keep track of daily homework assignments. Some teachers required the students to take them home and have their parents sign them every day, showing that the parents checked to make sure they followed through with the plan and completed their work. For some, these notebooks were an inconvenience; but for many, it was used as a way to keep communication open between school and home and to keep the students accountable for work they needed to complete. The purpose was to keep everyone on track with an actionable and measureable plan or road map—for the students, parents, and teachers.

For the students and parents who already understood the importance and benefit of being able to accomplish more under a system or process, this worked well. But for the children who were more disorganized—or perhaps didn't even care about their studies—it was likely a cause of frustration because it tended to show the truth. If they didn't follow the plan, they were more likely to miss homework or be unprepared for the coming day.

So now that we're all grown up, how does this apply to us? It applies to everyone to some extent or another. If you have a measurable starting point—a starting weight, an initial amount of money, or the time it took to complete a task—you can set a goal based on that and then make a plan to reach that goal. How do you reach that goal? By following the plan and then measuring your progress daily or weekly to make sure you are on track to reach the goal. As it is with any plan, adjustments may be needed if the proper progress is not made. But the only way to know that for sure is by measuring.

Think of anyone who has become very good or successful at something. Did it just magically happen? Despite natural gifts and talents, in most cases, no, it did not. There was something else behind it: tracking skills and progress.

Consider all the great athletes—whether they play baseball, golf, they swim, or do something else. The baseball players always know their runs-batted-in, earned run average, strikeouts, and batting averages. Golfers know their putting averages, driving accuracy percentage, and carry distance. They follow their statistics very closely and are continuously in competition to improve their scores as they strive for certain goals.

Did you read the book *Moneyball* by Michael Lewis or see the movie? It is a fantastic example of someone who set out to find out what positions individuals were good at playing. Once he had that information, he set up the team according to the positions that each person played well. By doing so, he was able to strategically lead

the team to a win. Billy Beane's idea of following the metrics data certainly didn't go over well with the conventional thoughts of what made a valuable baseball player; however, by doing exactly that, he was able to focus on the strong points of undervalued players and put together a winning team. Still today, the Oakland A's are a major league team with a payroll much, much less than the other major league teams.

How about one of the most common New Year's resolutions: losing weight? If a person who has had weight issues decides it's time to lose weight, usually the first thing they do is step on the scale to find out what they weigh—their starting point. Based on that, they set a goal, and then they make a plan to reach that goal. How do they reach that goal? By following the plan and then stepping back on the scale on a daily or weekly basis to make sure they are on track to reach their goal. As it is with any plan, adjustments may be needed if the proper progress is not made. But the only way to know that for sure is by measuring.

How about managing your bank account? Dave Ramsey, among many other financial advice people, says we should be able to account for every dollar we spend. A person who does this will build wealth. There are many other examples of measuring and managing; the bottom line is, as Charles Coonradt spells out in his book *The Game of Work*, "If you can't measure it, you can't manage it." A person who has set business goals and then has grown that business successfully and profitably is measuring. He or she is tracking certain data and then using that real data to make

decisions in order to take the business more easily in the direction in which it should go.

I've had the great pleasure of working with many small business owners, from the solopreneur to the owners of big multi-million-dollar businesses. It's hard to beat the great joy of watching, for example, a small business owner go from $2.5 million to $12.5 million in a couple years. He was able to go beyond his comfort zone and spend the time, effort, and money to figure out how to track all the important aspects of his business to see where he was weak and where he was strong. As a result of those efforts, he was able to improve the systems, processes, and placement of his people, thus bringing his company to greatly increased revenues.

Or how about a small business that was able to take their company overall closing percentage from 15% to 36% through the proper use of data? Or another business that was able to decrease marketing by 30% while increasing revenues by 17%? Or another business that had a tracking system for their people that provided a faster path to sales?

So, if people realize that goals cannot be managed if they can't be measured, why wouldn't all of them track? There could be many reasons, but probably the main reason is that people simply do not understand how much of a financial impact tracking has on a business, and the use of tracking (or lack thereof) can mean all the difference between a business dying, surviving, or thriving. Once that is understood, then the rest comes more easily.

There are other reasons, too, such as fear. That nasty four-letter word stops people every minute of every day! It is something that separates the successful from those who just don't quite make it in business or, in other words, fail. If you understand the profound impact tracking can have on your business, it's much easier to conquer that fear and do what is needed to grow your business profitably.

How about you? What are you tracking in your business? Income and expenses, I'm sure, as those are pretty easy to track—at least in the lump sums. Anyone can look at his or her bank account and see that this much was spent and this much came in. That's easy. How about beyond that? Are you able to look at the items that comprise your budget to see where money has been spent effectively or ineffectively? When you compare it to the budget you set out to meet, where are you? If you are off, are you able to see why and make the necessary adjustments going forward?

When planning a budget, there are certain costs and expenses that are predictable. For example, if you have a business that sells a product or service, more than likely you know exactly what it costs you to provide that service. Maybe the labor and material to complete the sale is 60% of your contract price. Then your salespeople need to get paid too, so 10% of the contract goes to pay commissions. If you have an office, insurance, electricity, and water bills, those bills need to get paid, so let's include 10% of the sale for those costs. That brings your fixed costs to 80%. Eighty percent of every sale you have made has and will go to getting the

job done. Those costs or expenses are not optional; they are fixed based on a percentage of sales.

There are two more major components of your budget that are NOT fixed: marketing and profits. *They can fluctuate enough to make the difference between your business making a profit or not.* Unfortunately, marketing has been one part of a budget that most people understand they need to spend money on, but it has often become that big, black hole of the unknown because the return on it has been so difficult to manage.

If your budget allows for 10% in marketing, your profit margin will be 10%. Because most of the items on your budget list are fixed and in direct proportion to sales, if you sell your products and services according to accurate price lists and overspend on your marketing, your profits are the only thing affected! That means if marketing expense percentages go up, profits go down. If marketing goes way up, then profits go way down! This is where the business owner feels the pain.

So how do you solve that problem? The solution used to be rather difficult and time-consuming, but now we are so fortunate to live in such a technological world and have all kinds of help available through specially designed systems. Since it is the business owner whose profits are most directly affected, it almost goes without saying that it's up to the owner to find a system that provides the numbers needed to grow a business profitably. Unfortunately, this decision is often left up to the salespeople, the receptionist, or a sales manager. This is backwards. A system that someone other

than an owner would pick out often focuses more on the fancy widgets, gadgets, features, and functions, but does not provide the revenue-producing numbers an owner needs to track leads, sales, and marketing unless a lot more time and money is invested in programming.

The choice of a lead, sales, and marketing tracking software must include those numbers that will be the milestones, the benchmarks, and the maps for growing revenues—the very numbers that allow a business owner to make the informed decisions necessary to grow a business profitably. Tracking doesn't have to be complicated. Lots of features and functions tend to lead to confusion, which lead to misuse or no use, so keep it simple! There are systems out there that are designed especially for the small- and medium-sized business owners to get the information they need in order to grow a business profitably as well as provide very nice CRM services for the salespeople, so do your homework.

While you are looking for systems to help you grow your business profitably, keep an eye out for certain data that should be included:

* Number of leads that came in during any period of time from all paid and unpaid advertising
* Lead cost per advertising source and total lead cost for all advertising sources combined
* Types of leads and geographical location per advertising source
* Number of leads that converted to sales
* Lead conversion timetable—leads to orders, orders to billable sales

* Individual conversion or closing ratio in comparison to company and industry standards and goals
* The percentage and actual dollar cost of getting a sale for each advertising source
* The cost of getting a sale for any salesperson for any advertising source
* Gross profits on dollars, including cost of sales
* Number of sales and dollar amount sold to previous customers, referrals, and other unpaid advertising
* Your salespeople's strengths and weaknesses for types of jobs sold compared to what your company offers

Using the data as suggested above will give you, the owner or manager, the data necessary to make daily decisions, thus empowering you to grow your business and reach your goals in a methodical, measured way. You will be able to easily see what is or is not working and have the power to train, change, or modify certain aspects within your business in order to keep on the path to reaching your goals.

So now going back to the beginning question, what's the difference between a dream and a goal? I prefer to say, "A goal is a dream with an actionable deadline." When you take the steps necessary to keep your business on track, your dream becomes actionable, and reaching your goal by the deadline becomes realistic. Winners know their numbers!

— ABOUT THE AUTHOR —

Susan Raisanen's background is in education, both as a teacher and principal. One summer she got hooked on Small Business America, and now she loves helping busy business owners and executives get the data they need to grow their business more profitably. Her company Profit Pro CRM provides a sales, lead, and marketing tracking system that was created out of an urgent need in her family's businesses. Having a lot of salespeople and spending a fortune on marketing, they needed to know what was working and what was not and needed a way to use that data to assign leads, add/subtract initiatives and people, and effectively execute sales and marketing. Visit Susan's website at http://www.profitfinderpro.com. She has a great tool for salespeople to determine the steps to reaching their goals at http://www.profitfinderpro.com/calculator.

CHAPTER 14

Building a Holistic Foundation for Business

By Dr. Laurén M. Laurino

"I am the master of my fate: I am the captain of my soul."
"Invictus," – William Ernest Henley

Thirteen years! You may have heard the saying, "Your work becomes your life." That was my mundane reality during my thirteen-year state career. Some crazy circumstances, combined with guidance from an old-school mindset brought me there and it took all that time for me to come to the realization I didn't have to stay. Are you stuck in a similar circumstance? You know that your current job or business isn't for you, but, just like me, for whatever reasons you have failed to do anything about it. Most of us have been there at one point in our lives. To just jump to another job is not the answer. Look inside of yourself. What is your burning desire? What excites you? What is your life's work?

For me, I chose to turn my backstory into a positive life by using my experience as a stepping-stone toward fully aligning with my destiny—pursuing holistic healing and business coaching. My own journey was exciting and I want to help you break free of the boring and mundane and breathe new life into your business and personal pursuits. You can rewrite your destiny!

"Holistic" is a word derived from the root word "holism" and characterizes comprehension of the parts to be interconnected and explicable only by reference to the whole the in the pursuit and achievement of balance. It allows you to gain fulfillment in all aspects of your life. When you integrate your personal life, work life, and spiritual life you can gain fulfillment in all aspects of your life.

The greater the fulfillment that you feel internally, the faster you'll attract your deepest desires to you. Every day, I practice the "You always get what you need when you need it" mantra. I set visionary goals (using a vision board) within specific timeframes, including fine details and recognizable landmarks while giving myself wiggle room and respecting the fact that I am human, and they work! There is no need to stress or be doubtful. It will work for you too as long as you trust and believe in yourself. It means going with the flow of your life's work instead of getting caught up just in business. In my holistic approach to business I take thoughts, physicality, and energy into account, I help others to develop an unbreakable and unbeatable business plan with a foundation on all levels.

Holistic entrepreneurs are in alignment with their passion and consciously create their life experience through vision. Their

work, love and life, are combined, NOT separated. A great chef once taught me how cooking is an art form. He explained that you must start by building your kitchen [foundation] in order to begin creating a palatable *masterpiece*. I observed his style of cooking as a way of creativity [mind] with ingredients as the physical component [body] while he was joyously tasting his food from time to time and tweaking the spices to get it right just as he envisioned it [spirit]. I enjoyed the way he effortlessly danced around the kitchen the entire time, exuding confidence and sometimes even singing in Italian. It was with this kitchen analogy in mind while trusting in my inner guidance that I began creating my dream job. Just so you know, your dream job may not exist. It can be that you'll have to create it. I tweaked and tailored my plans and actions along the way just like the chef did with his recipe until eventually I realized *my masterpiece* was to help others become a holistic entrepreneur.

What if you aligned your work or current business with *your* life's purpose? When you truly do what you love, you'll find more fulfillment than you could ever imagine. You'll experience the difference in every aspect of your life. It will have a positive effect on the relationships with your family and friends. Not only will your stress levels reduce and the feel-good hormones in your body like oxytocin and serotonin increase, on a spiritual level you'll experience more joy. The first step of your journey is to release these mood-enhancing endorphins: start by always being grateful. Next you need a vision.

Vision

Have you ever looked at a tool in the hardware store that you may have never seen before? If so, did your mind immediately begin making up uses for this tool? Let's pretend that you are in the aisle at your local hardware store, and you pick up a funky looking tool off of the shelf. You hold it up and twist it around, eyeing all of its sides and shapes. You start fantasizing about what you can accomplish with it. Then an old-timer comes walking down the aisle and asks you if you know what the tool your holding is used for. He proceeds to tell you and you are proud of yourself because its exact purpose did cross your mind, in addition to the myriad other tasks it could also be used for. You enthusiastically tell him that you figured out its main purpose, and you also thought it could be used for other things too! The old man furrows his brow and then raises it as if he is having his first ever visual revelation, saying, "Well, why didn't I think of that in the last fifty years?"

When you begin to create your vision, you need to think out of the box. Knowledge works best if you know where you are going. Look at all possibilities, not just the obvious ones. Take the time to research your dream. In this new age of business, we have access to information in a snap. When you have the right information and listen to your intuition, you can accelerate your success. By tapping into your creativity, you enable yourself to bypass many old-school setbacks and not fall into the same trap the old-timer did.

Try taking a yoga class or maybe some painting classes to get your creative juices flowing. Art and Wine classes are not a good

idea though, because you want to be clear and sober. A sketchpad or journal accessible 24/7 is vital. Write down everything that comes to mind: pictures, colors, textures, sounds, scenes, and even things that don't make any sense to you. Upon review of your chicken scratch you may be surprised of the great ideas you came up with. Try the exercise below to help define your vision.

Exercise: These are good questions to ask and then draw out the answers on your sketchpad. Be as specific, detailed, and colorful as possible.

✻ What is my core passion?

✻ What commonalities might my current or potential business have in line with my passion?

✻ What are some ways I can consider aligning my current business with my passion?

✻ How will I feel if my business and passion were aligned?

✻ How will this positively affect my market?

✻ What are the five things most important to me that I cannot live without?

✻ By aligning my business with my passion, do I see the five things most important to me included in my vision effortlessly?

✻ Is my ideal lifestyle now a byproduct of being fully empowered and doing what I love for life?

✻ What steps can I take to begin integrating my passion into my current business plan? Or what steps can I take to begin building my new business with the essence of my passion weaved into it?

You need to see it to believe it; and when you believe it, you can achieve it! Just like your favorite football team draws out all their tactics and strategies on a whiteboard, this sketchpad is your game plan. Each play is a step closer to victory, and each game's victory is a step closer to the big game. Each day the players are living, eating, and breathing their reality as champions. They are confident that if a strategy doesn't work, they can keep it in their toolbox but erase it off the board and draw a new one that better fits their intention to win a particular game. The potential for victory is always there; it's just a matter of applying knowledge, resources, and skill to your vision. The vision and trust in your inner guidance is what will help you to effortlessly pull up the play needed in the very nick of time - just make sure to stick to your first gut reaction. Energy is another key tool in developing your holistic business.

Energy

You may already be taking a holistic approach to business, but don't even recognize it.

You can make energy work for you—it's free. One form of energy you will certainly recognize comes from positive and upbeat people. The fact is everything is energy, even if it's disguised in a physical shape. Learning how to harness and transmute energy into your desires can be easy and effortless. Effortlessness is that easy feeling of going with the flow. And how can you not be going with the flow when you're doing what you love?

When you choose to be like water and flow around the rocks and debris that fall in your stream as opposed to becoming stagnant, life is blissful. In the same way, success and money will cruise to you. You will know that you are mastering the holistic business model, are taking the right actions and are in tune with yourself and your business, when you observe money pouring in at a steady, abundant flow. You will also find more meaning in setting, pursuing, and achieving any personal or professional goal.

Please know that my holistic business team and I are here to provide any guidance you may need and are very interested in featuring your success story, especially any business related visionary story, on www.drrenrecommends.com. For any holistic business inquiries or relatable matters regarding the information contained in this chapter, please contact me at: info@drrenrecommends.com.

ABOUT THE AUTHOR

Dr. Laurén M. Laurino, BCND lovingly known as "Dr. Ren, America's Naturopathic Sweetheart" is a Holistic Health Crusader from Union, New Jersey. She is a Board Certified Naturopathic Doctor thru the American Naturopathic Medical Board and the President of the New Jersey Holistic Chamber of Commerce. She can be reached for speaking events and consultations out of her offices in New York, Los Angeles and Headquarters located at the Phoenix Institute of Holistic Health and Research 100 Valley Rd, Montclair, NJ 07042. Contact: info@drrenrecommends.com (212) 335-0174 / (310) 775-2977 or toll free (844) 205-8733 Instagram: Dr_Ren. Facebook: https://www.facebook.com/drrenfanpage. Twitter: @laurenlaurino

<h2><h2>CHAPTER 15</h2></h2>

From Fear to Faith

By Zina Solomon

"Love is what we were born with. Fear is what we learned here."
— Marianne Williamson

One beautiful summer afternoon we were invited at a pool party of a family friend. Everyone was having a good time. Suddenly, someone screamed, "She's drowning! She's drowning!" I vaguely heard that voice, as if I were in a nightmare. Gasping for air, attempting to get out of the depths, I felt as though I was running out of time and life was passing me by. Everything seemed to fade gradually until a stranger jumped in and pulled me out from the pool. It was me who almost drowned. I was eleven years old and did not know how to swim.

Have you ever felt like you were drowning? Overwhelmed with despair and paralyzed? When anxiety, stress, nervousness, and fear take over your body, your mind shuts down and it's hard

to think logically. If, through this chaotic noise that is going on in your mind, you pause for a millisecond and listen to your inner guide, you'll know what to do to survive, and can thrive in your endeavors.

Has fear hindered you from growing personally or professionally? Are your fears keeping you from achieving your goals right now? Do not despair. You *can* overcome your fear; everyone is capable and worthy of it. The key is to push past fear, discover and explore that you have greatness and power within you, and then use it! Create an impact and find ways to serve others.

Since that episode years ago, the thought of swimming kept haunting me. The fear prevented me from engaging in water activities. I would observe my friends engaging in adventurous activities, such as an Ironman and triathlons, and I dreamt about overcoming that fear and learning to swim at an adult age.

"Setting goals is the first step in turning the invisible into the visible." – Tony Robbins

In early 2010, I set out to conquer my greatest fear. I registered in February for the Musselman Triathlon in Geneva, NY. This is a sprint triathlon consisting of a 750-meter swim, a 16.1-mile bike ride, and finally a 3.2-mile run. Since the event wasn't until mid July, I had plenty of time to learn how to swim and train. My goal was to complete the triathlon, and I refused to allow fear to be an obstacle against my dreams. I kept visualizing what it would be like to finish

the race and to swim with ease. I kept repeating that imagery in my mind as part of my mental preparedness and fortitude.

"Even the wildest dreams have to start somewhere.
Allow yourself the time and space to let your mind wander
and your imagination fly." – Oprah Winfrey

Do you have a dream that you have always wanted to pursue but allowed fear to steal away from you? Well, you can take it right back by first using your imagination to make it real for yourself and then making a plan of action. The first step in designing any action plan to follow a dream is to decide you will create a change. Then, set a date and take action to achieve that change.

The moment I decided to do the triathlon and committed to it by registering is when magic started to happen. Before I signed up, I did not have all the answers. I simply took a leap of faith, trusted that the answers would come, and allowed my courage and intuition to guide me. Failure was not an option, and I was committed to succeeding. I did not know how I was going to learn how to swim, but soon, opportunities started to unfold. I found the perfect coach, a friend who is a great triathlete.

This made me feel even more inspired to complete the race. I trained as much as I could and I ensured that every moment I invested in my training counted. During one training session in open water, I panicked and once again encountered a near drowning experience. Paralyzed by fear and in a state of hyperventilation, I

was rescued. I have to admit I wrestled with the thought of quitting. However, I decided not to give up. I was not going to allow fear to control my life.

When you have a burning desire and set a goal, you will find that you attract not only situations that align with your vision, but people who will help as well.

> *"The scariest moment is always just before you start."*
> *– Stephen King*

Before I knew it, it was July 10, 2010—the day of my very first triathlon. It was a beautiful, sunny morning. The air was fresh and crisp, the lake was beautiful, and I had butterflies in my stomach. Once the pistol was shot for my wave, everyone began to swim swiftly like dolphins and mermaids, and I was left behind. My fear was the next wave of swimmers would swim over me and that I would drown. I couldn't catch my breath, I felt overwhelmed and considered quitting once again. I had only a few seconds to decide whether I was going to get back in the game and complete the race or get out and get disqualified. I took several deep breaths. I had to trust and believe in myself and my abilities.

"You can do it!" I heard a voice say. It was as if an angel was talking to me. I looked around. It was one of the lifeguards. "You have an excellent stroke. Don't give up!" The moment I heard that, it reminded me of my purpose, and I completed 750 meters in twenty-five minutes and thirty-eight seconds. The hardest part was

over, and victory was within reach. Perseverance, determination, focus, persistence, and a split second decision-making made all the difference.

We all encounter obstacles in life. It's a matter of how we perceive them. Are we using these obstacles as roadblocks or as building blocks? If you are a runner or an athlete, you know what hitting the "wall" means. It's a point where you feel that you can no longer go any further. It is also at this point where endorphins kick in, and once you push through and continue to stay the course, you successfully complete the race. It's the same for any goal. It is only through perseverance that we accomplish anything.

"A vision is not just a picture of what could be; it is an appeal to our better selves, a call to become something more."
– Rosabeth Moss Kanter

Life Without Fear

Go back to thinking about that dream you had, and the fear that stood in your way. Do you have a fear that has paralyzed you for years and you have not yet overcome? Again, has it hindered you from growing in any way? Think about it for a moment. What is it? Now, write it down. It's important to remember it so you can take the proper steps to overcome that fear.

We all have fears. We may tell ourselves that we are not good enough or that we are not worthy. If you step back for a moment

and reflect, you will realize that we were all born with love, passion and power within us. The key to replacing fear with love is to unleash our inner greatness and move towards your dreams—you overcome fear with action.

Imagine your life without any limitations—a life where fear does not exist. How would you orchestrate and plan your life? Well, the first step in designing any action plan is deciding that you will create a change and then setting a goal to achieve it. When setting a goal, whether it is business, health, or financial, you have to have a bigger vision—a bigger picture—of why you want to accomplish that goal in the first place. Find your purpose, and then set your goals around that purpose.

Every year, I write down the top ten goals that I want to accomplish for that year. I also have quarterly goals related to fitness, health, business, and more. Goals are your GPS. That's why it's important to spend time to create the right goals, ones you really want to attain.

When you focus your attention on achieving your goal, you'll find that opportunities, situations, people, and circumstances will start to appear to assist you in achieving and completing it—just like an opportunity to learn to swim appeared after I signed up for the race. By visualizing the picture of your dreams in your mind and focusing on the end result you'll start attracting situations and people who will be aligned with your vision.

Hire coaches and mentors to assist you in achieving certain goals. When I was randomly selected to run the New York City

Marathon in 2009, I hired a running coach to assist me in the training process. Hiring a coach or an expert is instrumental to taking your skills to the next level and attaining your success. Achieving your goals also means consistently exercising your talents and skills.

There are synergies among athletes and business owners. The synergy is this: input = output. What I mean by this is what you put in—your effort—will result in the output, or outcome, you desire. For example, if you train consistently for a race and continue to push through each wall you hit, you will achieve peak performance. But, if you don't use it, you lose it. Engaging your muscles in physical activity consistently strengthens it, but the lack of activity causes the muscles to weaken and decline. The same concept applies to business. When you put in the effort to create, design, and map out your business strategy, you will ultimately produce great results. When there is insufficient effort, the business fails. It's a matter of persistence, focus, consistency, perseverance, and dedication. It boils down to having the mental discipline to stay focused on course and not deviate from your goal and vision or give up.

"Every great dream begins with a dreamer. Always remember, you have within you the strength, the patience, and the passion to reach for the stars to change the world." – Harriet Tubman

Care for Your Body

It is your duty to take care of your body, and it's an important part of achieving your goals. Many people struggle with weight loss, energy, achieving peak athletic performance, and youthful aging. They struggle with releasing visceral fat, also known as belly fat. This breaks my heart because these struggles negatively impact their lives dramatically and makes it so much harder for them to focus on their dreams. I've created a free ten-minute training video to help you learn more about the causes of belly fat and how to address it. You can access this free training video by emailing freeoffer@zinasolomon.com. I'm also offering a free thirty-minute coaching consultation. To request a consultation, send an email to coaching@zinasolomon.com. We will schedule a time that is mutually convenient. Feel free to connect with me on social media (Facebook, LinkedIn, Twitter, Instagram, Pinterest, etc.).

Physical training and exercise may not seem to relate directly to attaining your goals, especially if those goals don't deal with your body, but trust me, taking care of your health and fitness helps. When you take care of yourself, you feel better, are less depressed and anxious, and have more energy to serve others and create the impact you desire.

Let yourself shine! Remember that you can do the most amazing things when you believe in yourself and visualize your goals. You have greatness inside you. Explore and discover your true talents and set them free! The more people harness their inner greatness and actively overcome fear, the more the world will shine.

— ABOUT THE AUTHOR —

Zina Solomon empowers artists and entrepreneurs to take charge of their health while having fun in the process. Zina assists her clients with increasing energy, releasing excess weight, having a clear mind, and more. Zina is certified in personal training, nutrition, and social media. She holds a master's degree from Rutgers University in human resource management. She has extensive experience in fitness, business strategy, coaching, social media, and consulting. Zina is a half marathon runner who is currently pursuing her passion of health & social media coaching and working in TV commercials and voice over projects. www.ZinaSolomon.com

CHAPTER 16

It's Not Over Until You Win

By Les Brown

> *"Life is God's gift. What we do with it is our gift to God."*
> *– Author unknown*

*W*hen the doctor called, I was expecting to hear that my results were fine. After all, I had only gotten a check-up to set an example for others, as part of a prostate cancer awareness program I supported. I didn't have pain or any complaints.

"Mr. Brown," the doctor said in a friendly voice. "I would like you to come in, so we can talk about your results." That's when I knew something was wrong. I insisted that he tell me over the phone, and he did. At that moment, I felt the ground was crumbling under my feet. Me? Prostate cancer? How was that possible? I was eating healthy, and I was a positive thinker. I couldn't help but think of all the things I still wanted to do. I

wanted to see my grandchildren grow up. I wanted to continue to motivate and inspire others. Why did this happen to me?

Trust me, that's not a good question to ask, because it doesn't get you anywhere. It distracts you from doing what is necessary to survive and truly live. Being afraid or wallowing in self-pity will prevent you from clearly seeing what actions to take. Easy is not an option.

It can be frightening to face the reality, but it's called life. I often say, "If things go wrong, don't go with them." I told myself, "It's possible that I can survive if I take charge of my mind, heart, and spirit." When you are facing a life-threatening disease, you don't have the luxury of feeling sorry for yourself. Get busy. Get into fighting mode. Don't surrender. I believe that life is a fight for territory. Once you stop fighting for what you want, what you don't want automatically takes over. You have to stand up and force yourself to take action. I had a loving, supportive partner, and she told me, "You are going to beat this." I adopted a plant-based diet. I used both traditional medicine and alternative methods. I prayed, meditated, exercised, and stayed away from negative people and anything that would create drama or stress in my life. I started living like Iyanla Vanzant recommended:

"Give to yourself until your cup runneth over,
then give to others from the overflow."

Fighting cancer gave me the opportunity to become more responsible, enlightened, and empowered. The lessons I've learned

can be applied to any goal you want to achieve, regardless of whether you are dealing with a life-threatening disease, financial or career difficulties, or family problems.

* **Take responsibility:** Do your research. Stay in communication with your doctor or health care professional. Find someone who is experienced to help you navigate the healthcare system. Become knowledgeable; find out what you have to do. Get actively involved by asking people questions and reading books. Carve out time to create rituals to forgive yourself and others who might have hurt you. Forgiving is not forgetting; forgiving is remembering without anger. Just as resentment can poison your system, so can fear. Being afraid won't do you any good, and fear will prevent you from seeing clearly. If you do what is easy, give up, surrender, or become fatalistic—your life will be hard. But if you do what is hard, encourage yourself in spite of, create inner peace, and think positive, your life will be easier. All of us are going to leave here someday; nobody has figured out how to get out of life alive. Let's stay as long as we can, be healthy, have lots of fun, and share love and laughter.

* **Walk in faith:** Tell yourself, "No matter how hard it is, I am going to make it." No matter how deadly your situation may appear, don't judge by appearances. Many people die, not from their disease, but from their own fatalistic thinking. They surrender and give up. There are studies that show that more people die from their doctor's prognosis than from the disease itself. I strongly believe that doctors should never

tell someone that he or she is terminally ill. Instead, they should say, "My ability to help you has terminated. You need to explore other options." Remember, life happens to all of us. That doesn't mean you are denying the facts—you are defying them. If life knocks you down, try to land on your back, because if you can look up, you can get up.

✴ **Build your belief:** Read stories about other people who have overcome the challenge you are dealing with. Become a voice of hope and inspiration to others if at all possible; it will build you up as well. Become part of a spiritual community that will strengthen you mentally, emotionally, and spiritually. You have to believe in your heart of hearts that it's possible to win, and you have to nurture that feeling. There are many diseases that have been called incurable, but people who were willing to do the work have been healed. Having the mindset that you expect to get better is very important in activating the healing process of your body. Discipline yourself to embrace a ritual of writing "as if" healing affirmations every day that call forth that what you want to achieve in your body. An example of a healing affirmations would be, "I give thanks that I am totally and completely healed." Affirm to yourself as you exercise or meditate: "I'm getting stronger. I'm getting better. I give thanks that I've gotten through this healing journey." Create positive healing relationships; encourage and support each other. Keep a journal. Read and listen to things that make you feel good, things that are positive and encouraging.

* **Decide to win:** There is nothing as powerful as a mind that has been made up. It has been said that every challenge we face is an opportunity for us to discover the spiritual part of ourselves that will allow us to rise above the situation. Take time every day to express gratitude and to visualize yourself being victorious, living a healthy, happy, and prosperous life. Make a conscious, deliberate effort to hold an optimistic view of the future. In The Dynamic Laws of Healing, I read a story of two men who went to the doctor for a physical exam. One was told that his health was great, and he lived for another twenty to thirty years. The other man was told that he was suffering from a terminal illness, and that he should get his affairs in order because he only had two or three months to live. Sure enough, he died within three months. Years later, the doctors discovered that because of a clerical error, the files had been switched. The moral of this story is: your attitude will decide your outcome. If you think you will lose, you will. If you decide to win, then you will win.

* **Laugh:** Hang out with people who make you laugh and bring you joy. You've got to have a sense of humor. Learn to laugh at yourself. Sometimes, you'll have to laugh just to keep yourself from crying and going crazy. Did you know that one minute of anger weakens your immune system for four to five hours? Did you also know that one minute of laughter boosts your immune system for over twenty-four hours? Don't let the little kid within you die just because you

are facing difficulties. Laugh your way through. Watch a lot of funny movies, read funny books, and keep your mood up. It can save your life.

* **Take care of your body:** If you feel great, you'll be more successful in life. Make sure you get proper rest and sleep, because sleep is a major factor in the healing process. In the middle of the night, your body repairs, rebuilds, and heals itself. People who have had radical remissions did several things. They ate a plant-based diet and stopped eating meat, dairy, sugar, and processed foods. They exercised. They also had social support. Make choices that indicate to your body that you expect to be around for years to come. I eat 80% organic fruits and vegetables and drink lots of alkalized water. I pray and meditate. Nothing tastes as good as great health feels.

* **Love and surround yourself with love:** Love the people around you and express your love to them. Many times when I was in physical pain, my anxiety, fears, and physical discomfort were reduced by getting involved in other things—especially speaking, helping and inspiring others—instead of being focused on myself. Find goals you can immerse yourself in. Give away your love, support, and energy. Create a healing environment that supports you and makes you feel your best. Eliminate clutter. Play soothing music that calms your spirit. Don't watch anything that is violent or creates stress in your life. Take baths with essential oils (like lavender), candles, and flowers. You may have to detoxify your life and remove the

negative, toxic people who could send you to an early grave. Be aware of the emotional vampires in your world who will suck the life out of you if you allow it. "Relational illness" is a new term in psychiatry that proves that some people can actually make you sick. There are nourishing relationships and toxic relationships: nourishing relationships can literally strengthen your immune system and influence your attitudes about yourself and your possibilities for your future, while toxic relationships drain you.

The most important lesson I learned was from my mentor. He told me, "Les, you are going to die."

I was shocked. "Why are you saying that, Mike?"

"Well," he said, "You're running around, scrambling, afraid that you are going to die. What you should be doing is asking yourself what the purpose of your life is. What is your reason for being here? Tell me, what will be different because you are here? What is your assignment? If you know your why for living, you can find a how."

He was right. I had to find a cause greater than myself. Once I was clear on the purpose I had to fulfill, it gave me hope for the future and power in the present. Getting actively involved in something that resonates with your spirit gives your life a sense of meaning and purpose. It will empower you to achieve your goals despite your own challenges. Being out of alignment with your purpose might create dis-ease in your body.

Imagine you are laying on your deathbed. Your goals, gifts,

abilities, dreams, and talents stand around you. They say, "We came to you. You never gave us life. Now, we must die with you forever." If you died today, which talents and dreams would die with you? What are the dreams you never pursued, the talents you never used? You likely have not even scraped the surface of your abilities. Focus on your strengths, not on your weaknesses and the things you have lost. Make the adjustment and move on. Do what you can with what you have going for you. Live full and die empty! Despite your current situation or circumstances, you have greatness within you. You are still here. You have a lot to be thankful for.

I'd like to tell you that it's easy—that you can easily think positive, and everything will be all right. The reality is that it's hard. It's hard taking a variety of painkillers that can provide welcome relief, but can also leave you lethargic, tired, and depressed. There were many times when I was hurting and just wanted a good night's sleep. It's not easy. It's hard to stay motivated and encouraged, to get up every day and keep your spirits up despite the feeling that death is watching over you. It's hard when you are worried about your family, your bills, and your responsibilities. It's hard; Easy is not an option. In life and in business, there are going to be ups and downs. I strongly believe that where there is a will, there is a way for you to produce miracles in your life. I've seen many people who have been given up on, but they get up and go on and live happy, productive lives. Keep the faith. Stand up within yourself. Your goal is worth fighting for! Never give up! It's worth it, and you can do it! I can tell you from my own experience that there is a

power and presence in you that is greater than your circumstances and greater than any disease you might be facing. Get still. Pray. Meditate. Visualize yourself being healed. Whatever life throws at you, cry out if you must, yet hold on to your faith, keep your head up, and say to life, "It's not over until I win."

— ABOUT THE AUTHOR —

Les Brown is one of the world's most renowned motivational speakers and speakers' coach. Les came up the hard way. He and his brother were adopted at the age of six weeks by a single woman, and raised in the Liberty City section of Miami, Florida. Les failed twice in school. In spite of these conditions, he became a popular radio personality and a community activist. He later served three terms in the Ohio State Legislature, becoming chairman of its Human Resources and Education Committee. He has had five PBS television specials, and had a nationally syndicated talk show produced by King World. He received the highest reward of the National Speakers Association, was selected by Toastmasters as one of the top five speakers in the world, and won the Golden Gavel Award in 1992. Learn more at www.LesBrown.com.

CHAPTER 17

Magnificent Promises

By Joyce Hack

> *"The greatest danger for most of us is not that our aim is too high, and that we miss it. The greatest danger is that our aim is too low and we reach it."* – Michelangelo

"Come on, Tiffany my darling, let's say a prayer and have lunch," I told my six-year-old daughter while putting her little sister Tammy in a chair.

"But Daddy isn't home yet," she replied while she ran to the big front window to see if she could spy her father's car pull up into the driveway.

"I know, sweetheart. He'll probably be home any minute. Let's have something to eat," I said, trying to reassure myself at the same time. It was unusual for Elmer to be this late and not call. *"There must be an emergency at the hospital that needs his attention,"* I thought to calm down my racing mind. Elmer was always willing

to help whenever and however he could, no matter how busy and hectic the night might have been. He would find time to let you know he cared.

"Trrrriinnng…" The phone startled me from my thoughts. When I answered, the voice on the other line said, "Good afternoon, ma'am. Are you Mrs. Hack?"

"Yes, who am I speaking with?"

"My name is Officer Brandy with the LAPD. I'm sorry, ma'am, but I have bad news for you. Your husband is in the intensive care unit of the Desert Hospital in Palm Springs. He was involved in a car accident, and he is in critical condition. When he arrived at the hospital, he was dead, but they revived him. Can you get someone to go with you to the hospital? Please don't go to the hospital by yourself."

During that thirty-second phone call, my life collapsed. Elmer was more than my husband—he was my soul mate, my best friend, the love of my life, and a great father for my daughters. What would I do without him? A friend came to watch my girls, and a couple from my church took me to the hospital. All I could do was pray, but I was too late. When we arrived at the hospital, an older doctor came over and caringly held my hand. "I am sorry, Mrs. Hack. Your husband has passed away."

"No, no, this can't be true! Not my dear Elmer!" I started crying and couldn't stop.

There are no words to describe the devastation and the pain as the reality started to creep in the next morning. My dear Elmer

would never come home again. How was I going to provide for my little girls? How would I make the next mortgage payment so we could stay in the house we bought just two months ago? How could I achieve our goal to provide them with opportunities and education without Elmer?

"Each of us is born with the freedom to dream to create a life we love and make every area in our life extraordinary."
– Joyce Hack

Elmer and I had worked together as a team toward our goals, and together we had created a life we loved. While he was in nursing school, I worked two jobs to support us. We had just made the adventurous move to Redlands, California, from Canada, allowing me to get my nutrition degree at Lomalinda University. Together we were going to make every area of our life extraordinary. Then this tragedy hit, and there was no more "together." It was just me with our precious daughters, two-year-old Tammy and six-year-old Tiffany. The love for my girls gave me a purpose to live and the strength to redesign my life's plan.

"Turn your wounds into wisdom." – Oprah Winfrey

No matter what obstacles you'll have to overcome, always remember that it's not over until you win. We all hit hard times and have to deal with defeats and tragedies—don't let that stop

you. Instead, turn every obstacle into a gift—an opportunity to grow, learn, and become a better and stronger person. Focus on your goals, not on the pain. It has not been an easy journey for me. Much like an architect, I had to go back to the drawing board and write out my plans to build a new life filled with promises.

Transform Your Goals into Promises

A promise is more powerful than a goal because it carries with it a much deeper sense of responsibility. Isn't it true that you take your promises much more seriously than a goal? The first step is to clearly identify the promise you want to make, just like you can't buy a flight if you don't know your destination. Make sure they are exciting and meaningful to you. That way, you are motivated and want to take action to make them come true.

Stay Focused

When life gets busy, it's easy to get caught up in it. When you keep your promise in sight, you'll stay focused on what you are creating. Put your life promises on paper in the present tense and read them daily. A good way to keep your promises on your mind is to make what I call a pocket promise. A pocket promise is a small laminated paper (the size of a business card) with your promises printed on the card. Once you have your promises printed on the card, print a dozen and have them laminated. Carrying the pocket promise each day will serve as a constant reminder of your promise. You can always have other visual reminders like index cards, photos, and posters in places you see often.

Coming in contact with your promise several times during the day will keep it fresh in your mind and will cause you to focus on it.

Have Faith

Make promises you can believe in. Have faith in yourself, in God, and in the incredible future in front of you, even if at times you have no idea how things will ever work out. Pray for guidance and give thanks for your blessings. My faith in God has carried me through. I knew that He would look after me and help me achieve my promises, just like it says in this beautiful poem:

The Rose

It is only a tiny rosebud
A flower of God's design.
But I cannot unfold the petals
With these clumsy hands of mine.

The Secret of unfolding flowers
Is not known to such as I.
The flowers of God opens so sweetly
In my hands would fade and die.

If I cannot unfold a rosebud
This flower of God's design,
Then how can I think I have wisdom
To unfold this life of mine?

So I'll trust Him for His leading
Each moment of every day,
And I'll look to Him for His guidance
Each step of the pilgrim way.

For the pathway that lies before me
My heavenly Father knows.
I'll trust Him to unfold the moments
Just as He unfolds the rose.

– John Denmark

Your Promise Should Fulfill Your Deepest Desire

Make sure that your promise is what *you* truly want. So many people go through life trying to make others happy and are never happy themselves. Your life is all you have and all you are, so why give it away? You may try to mold your goals to fit in with the masses, but that won't allow you to make a difference. Forget peer pressure, know what it is you truly want, and go after it. Don't waste your gifts and talents, and stay away from negative people who will hold you back.

Give It Your All

Go after your promise with a sense of urgency so that not even a minute is wasted. Don't find excuses why you can't do something. Believe that you can accomplish your promise and do whatever

it takes to make it happen. Your confidence in yourself will grow when you achieve smaller goals on the way to your bigger dreams.

To accomplish my promise of getting my education, I had to give it my all. Often I was up studying till three a.m. Thanks to my wonderful twin sister Joan, who helped me with my girls, and the willingness of the professors and my employer to work with me, I could continue going to school. When I graduated, I felt proud of myself and experienced a newfound sense of confidence. With this confidence, I continued to rebuild my life. I'm so grateful to my dear sister that she was there for me. I don't know what I would have done without her. She became like a second mom for my daughters and carried me through, so I could focus on study and school. To this day, she continues to be there for others. Her heart is filled with joy when she brings a smile to someone's day.

It's Not Over Until You Win

Don't allow a tragedy to overwhelm your desire to live, but see beyond the hurt and the heartbreak. You are the creator of your life—so live it! If you have been knocked down by life, acknowledge the setback and then take a leap ahead. If you keep your integrity, have a loving heart, and want to make a difference: you'll be successful, and great things will happen to you. You can make your dreams come true and keep your magnificent promises. Remember that it's not over until you win!

"Success is a peace of mind, which is a direct result of satisfaction in knowing you made the best effort to become the best you. The best you are capable of." – John Wooden

— ABOUT THE AUTHOR —

Joyce Hack is a clinical dietitian and health coach with over thirty years of experience. She has been called the "secret ingredient in a recipe for inspiration." She is an effective leader and is committed to positive outcomes in all aspects of life. She inspires others by her thoughtfulness and kindness.

Her passion is to encourage people to improve their lifestyle and health, inspiring them to live life powerfully. She has two precious daughters and two adorable grandchildren, and she loves collecting Victorian antiques. Visit her websites: www.9909244.fgxpress.com and www.5linx.net/joyceh or call 909-260-4234.

CHAPTER 18

Listen to Your Inner Voice

By Carol Metz Murray

"I like to listen. I have learned a great deal from listening carefully. Most people never listen."- Ernest Hemingway

ave you ever been so determined to achieve your goals that you refuse to listen to the subtle knocks at your door that are trying to tell you something is wrong? Have there been times where you ignored the knocks—pretending you never heard the sound? Opening the door and confronting reality would mean taking a deeper look at yourself—it could mean changes, forcing you to reevaluate your life and current goals. Eventually, the knocks get louder, but as long as you keep busy enough, you can still ignore them. Only when the door bursts open—or worse, when the roof falls on your head—are you finally stopped dead in your tracks. You can no longer run away, and you are forced to face what is really happening. Has this ever happened to you?

In my case, I wasn't listening to the soft knocks, let alone the louder ones. I was a single mom working hard at a full-time job as a city manager while traveling every other weekend for four to five hours (about 1,000 kilometers, 620 miles round trip) to attend university classes for my master's degree. I would leave Friday night and not return home until Sunday night.

It was my dream; when the opportunity presented itself, I had to go for it. I knew it was going to be a sacrifice, but I wanted to do it anyway. I was in bad shape physically, not exercising as my body called for, but I was determined to achieve my goals and refused to listen to the signals of my body. Some days, just putting one foot in front of the other was an effort. I was a mess emotionally and mentally as well as physically. I hadn't dealt with the unresolved issues from the abusive marriage I had recently escaped from.

I didn't pay attention to any of the signs. One day, I could almost hear a voice saying, "Well, Carol, if you're not going to listen, I'll have to get your attention another way." When my doctor told me that she would admit me to the hospital if I didn't take a leave of absence, I was terrified. I hated the thought of being admitted to a hospital just as much as I hated the thought of having to miss work and stay at home. Even though my body desperately needed a rest both mentally and physically, I took the leave kicking and screaming. It wasn't easy to tell my boss, the mayor of the city, that I needed to take an extended leave of absence. You see, I loved my job. It was exhilarating, and it gave me a sense of fulfillment—but it had taken its toll on me.

I tried to find the positives in taking this time off. I figured that I would be giving my body, mind, and spirit time to heal, and I would also be able to focus on writing my thesis. Have you ever found yourself in a situation like this? You have a deadline looming, but you are so exhausted that the thought of doing *anything* is daunting? Despite my mental state and physical health, I pushed myself to finish my thesis, and I was able to grind it out before the deadline.

With excitement and a feeling of relief, I faxed my thesis to the University of Southeast Alaska, and I walked across the hallway with a sense of healthy pride. I was getting ready to enjoy a well-deserved celebration for my great accomplishment. As I walked by the newspaper stand, I picked up a copy of the *Whitehorse Star*, the local newspaper. Somehow, it just kind of fell open to the page I needed to see. In a split second, my joy had turned into shock. I couldn't believe what I saw! I looked again to make sure I read it correctly—and unfortunately I had. That job posting turned my life upside down.

The city I used to work for was looking for a city manager. That's right—that was *my* job! After the long, excruciating hours I had worked in the office—sacrificing my health, giving up precious time I could have spent with my daughter, and so much more—there was my job being advertised? I was shocked and angry! That was the one and only graduation gift I received for completing my master's program—*unemployment*. There was no time to cry and get emotional about it. I had to pull myself

together—and quick. I had a daughter to raise, I still needed to take care of my health, and I needed to find a new place to live in the middle of the winter because the house I was renting from the city was part of my employment package. In that moment, the rug was pulled out from underneath my feet. Yet, this knock at the door turned out to be a valuable gift. It became a turning point in my life. Because of this moment, I gained the courage and motivation to start my own consulting company. It had been my dream; so when the opportunity presented itself, I had to go for it. I knew it was going to be a sacrifice, but I wanted to do it anyway.

The lessons I've learned in the process of transitioning from an unemployed, single mom to a successful business professional are very profound:

* **Know that a larger purpose is unfolding in you.** There is a reason for the knocks on your door. When you stop to listen and look within yourself, you'll discover much about yourself. Face what is in front of you and accept responsibility. Everything you do impacts you either positively or negatively, whether it's the food you eat, the stresses you put on yourself, or the emotions you choose to not deal with. In my case, I had some mountains to climb to get my health back in shape, but I learned to respect and honor the body I was given. I learned to listen; and by doing that, I found my purpose.

* **Achieving a goal is always possible even amidst adversity.** Being focused on your goal allows you to keep moving forward. Tap into your internal strength and know that you will get through

whatever circumstance you are faced with. I was committed and laser-focused on completing my master's degree in public administration. Every day, I would do a little bit of work on my thesis. It was tough because I was just so exhausted—mentally, emotionally, and physically—but I did it.

* **Fuel your desire.** Open up to the desire inside yourself and express it fully. It's who you are. Get out of your own way and allow great things happen. Whenever you face difficulties, tap into your desire and inner strength and believe in yourself no matter what.

* **Hold the space by really believing that it's going to happen.** "Holding the space" isn't just a bunch of words. You have to take the dream inside of you and keep working toward it until you reach it. The stronger your intention is, the faster things will happen. Never give up on yourself, regardless of the transition you are going through or how long it takes to achieve your dream. When you unlock your unlimited human potential, you'll unleash your inner power.

* **Build courage.** You need courage to go after your dreams. Having family, friends, and mentors support you along the way helps to build your courage. When I was struck with the devastation of having to move to escape my husband, only to find myself unemployed and without a home, I was grateful that I had the support of my daughter and friends. Courage gives strength to persevere.

Eventually my journey led me to a crossroad, and I made the decision to change and listen to that knock at the door. Because of the challenges I faced and the person I became, I've had the privilege to help people and companies be successful in their own transitions. I can help you, too!

— ABOUT THE AUTHOR —

Carol Metz Murray is a spiritual entrepreneur, business mentor, consultant, and speaker. She teaches entrepreneurs how to organize and implement business strategies and build wealth. Carol lives her life's purpose by being the change she wants to see in the world while removing limitations on her personal growth through continuous self-evaluation. Her leadership background of over twenty years with businesses, a non-profit organization, and city government provides her with extremely diverse and rich experiences. Contact her to open doors and discover your true potential. Learn more on her website: www.carolmetzmurray.com.

CHAPTER 19

Happy are Those Who Dream and Take Action Wholeheartedly

by Jeanna Brown

"It always seems impossible until it is done." – Nelson Mandela

hen I was in fifth grade, my mother enrolled me into a program called PJ's Concepts. It was a modeling/ etiquette school for young people from age eight to eighteen. Little did she know what a profound impact PJ's would have on my life. The program was so much more than the fundamentals of how to act. My mentor taught me to dream. No, I was taught to dream big! It was at PJ's that I learned how to focus those dreams, set goals and achieve them. Everything else was icing on the cake.

While still in school I redirected my focus to getting good grades, playing sports, graduating, and getting a college education. After completing my degree, my goal was to ultimately have a great career and have my own business ideally. As a business owner, I

knew you could make your own decisions and control your income to unlimited heights (or lows) with no ceiling or waiting for the boss to promote you.

I truly believe I owe my success to PJ's because it taught me that I was allowed to dream big from an early age. It gave me great mentors and amazing influencers. Key achievements in my life are a direct result of setting goals and learning how to set a plan in place at a young age. As PJ's had such a powerful impact on my life, it inspired me to create a confidence building program for professional women called *Develop U,* that is changing lives and modeled after PJ's. By teaching professional women regardless of where they are in their career, soft skills like business etiquette, clear and concise communication skills, as well as runway modeling, they become more assertive, and are better equipped to deal with any situations whether at home or at work. Along the way, I also learned why some people would get things done and others would not.

Through my childhood and the success I've experienced now, I've found that there are three main elements needed to achieve the goals you set for yourself:

1 **Write your goals down.** It goes without saying, but I need to say it: first, you need a goal. You need to dream really big. Once you have at least one, write your goal(s) down. Every successful person alive shares that common attribute. Every coach, teacher, and so many others have an objective and a goal. So do you, so write it down right now. Whether you're a teenager or a retiree—always write your goals down.

Break down your major, long-term goals into quarterly, monthly, weekly, and daily goals. Your goals should be measurable and have a deadline. You should also come up with the reason why you want to achieve these goals. Do not—I repeat—do not leave the why part out. It's like not adding apples to an apple pie. It is a critical ingredient. If your why doesn't align with your vision or isn't something that matters to you, then you won't succeed because you won't be motivated.

Then, determine how you are going to achieve your goals. Remember to be realistic about what you can get done. Your goals should be doable. Your goals shouldn't be to go from $100 in the bank to $40 million in a year. Finally, figure out who you are going to be accountable to. Who is your watch guard?

2 **Stay focused on your plan.** There are many tracks we can go down, and we often end up on tracks that are not in the playbook and that won't help us achieve our goals. Often, we have no idea how we got over there. Some colorful distraction came marching down the road, and we take a detour. Who told us to do that? We look around, and we're not quite sure who told us to go down this track but we know we followed something that was not specifically right for us. It happens. Be aware of it and try to counter it.

Look at your playbook—that goal list you just wrote out. What did you say you wanted to achieve? By when? Why? Look at your list and regroup. Reset new deadlines and go for it. Do not dwell on the stuff you did not do. Re-commit to

yourself and, if need be, to those affected by you accomplishing the goal. Then, keep pushing forward. Trust your plan and see it through.

3 **Celebrate.** So what do you do once you have reached your goal? Many of us get lost in this area right here. Once I finished college, the biggest goal in my life at the time, I didn't know what to do. I did not have a playbook for after college. For most of us, we were taught to get a good job, stay for thirty-five years, and retire. That was not the path for me.

Once you reach your goal, celebrate and reward yourself. Give yourself accolades of achievement and the permission to be great. Our society does not reward greatness outside of awards shows and sports competitions, so you have to celebrate yourself for you. If it is uncomfortable for you, which it probably will be, you should get your external support system to assist you. Simply tell them what you are working toward and that once you achieve it, you plan to do, buy, or eat XYZ. What you need them to help you with is to make sure you actually reward yourself. This helps you two-fold. At this point, you have not achieved the goal yet. So, your built in accountability partner is going to keep asking you, "Did you finish your goal?" You are really going to want that reward, and you won't want to let the other person down by saying you did not do it because you did not feel like it. It does not matter how great or small because the result is the same. You achieved. Once you're finished celebrating, set another goal.

There was a wildly successful advertising phrase for a shampoo that gave the instructions "Shampoo, rinse and repeat." That's my best advice for you. Dream big. Set realistic, doable goals that you have a burning desire to reach. Stay focused and do not let anything deter you from reaching your goal. Celebrate your success and repeat!

— ABOUT THE AUTHOR —

Jeanna Brown is a successful entrepreneur and motivational coach. Her coaching, training, and speaking for the past twenty-plus years has encouraged and motivated hundreds of women. She is the founder of *Develop U*, an interactive, comprehensive confidence-building program for professional women. She is also an author and the radio host of "Ladies Let's Talk with Coach Jeanna" on www.blogtalkradio.com/coachjeanna. Jeanna is passionate about helping others realize their dreams and potential by using the fundamentals of life. To work with any of her systems, go to her website www.CoachJeanna.com or call 866-521-1349.

CHAPTER 20

The Dream Achiever

By Elizabeth Bress-VonderHaar

"Dare to achieve your dreams." – Elizabeth Bress-VonderHaar

It was hard to open my eyes, and I felt extremely exhausted. My body was in excruciating pain like I was trapped in a body that wasn't mine. I noticed my mom was holding my hand. Distant voices were talking, but I couldn't understand what they were saying. It just sounded like a lot of noise. I felt my mom kissing me, but my only thought was to get this uncomfortable brace off my leg. Then, I saw a doctor next to my bed. He said with a Portuguese accent, "Como se sente menina? (How are you feeling little girl?") I didn't respond. I was numb from the medication and couldn't remember what happened. My mind was racing. Why was I in a hospital bed? I started screaming, "Mami, Mami! I have a terrible pain in my foot. Please take off this brace!"

My mother calmed me down and said, "It's okay, sweetheart. Your body needs time to heal. You've been in surgery for six hours." Slowly, it all started to come back to me. My family had made huge sacrifices for me to have this surgery because in Bolivia where I'm from, we don't have good health insurance. We found out through a friend that one of the best traumatology surgeons was working in San Pablo, Brazil and he would operate free of charge since I would be an interesting case study for his hospital. My parents saved for months and borrowed money once again to pay for the hospital bills, the travel expenses, and accommodations for me to recover after the surgery. My sixteen-year-old sister Marisol, my mom, and I lived in a hotel for three and a half months while my fifteen-year-old sister and my youngest sibling, who was only two at that time, stayed with my dad.

The doctor pulled away the sheets, and suddenly, what happened fully hit me. My leg! My leg was hurting so bad, yet it wasn't there anymore. My leg had been amputated, and the pain was phantom pain. After seven unsuccessful surgeries throughout my childhood and because of my inability to walk without the help of an eight-pound orthotic, I had decided at the age of eleven to have my limb amputated. Being born there with a congenital disorder that left me without a fibula in my right leg was very difficult. The lack of awareness for people with disabilities made my life a constant struggle. Amputating my leg would allow me to get a prosthetic limb so I could look a little more like the other children. That was my biggest dream.

The doctor said, "You are a brave young lady. It may still be painful for a couple of weeks, but the wound should start healing in about fifteen days." Little did I know how much pain I would have to suffer. Soon after, I developed gangrene. My leg's body tissue was dying (necrosis), which affected my blood circulation, allowing bacteria to spread and causing infection in my amputated leg. In addition, the doctors diagnosed me with a skin condition called Keloid that doesn't allow the skin to heal properly. It was a nightmare. The wound kept bleeding, and pus wouldn't stop coming out. After three days in the hospital, I was released, but I had to come back every day to have the dead cells removed without anesthesia for three months—and those three months felt like an eternity! The pain was so intense that to this day, I can barely remember that time even though it marked my life forever.

Focusing on my goal—my dream of getting a prosthetic limb—helped me endure the intense physical pain. After four weeks, however, the wound was still not healing, and the doctors told my mother that I would need another amputation. But there was no money for another surgery and the additional expenses we would incur. Fortunately, a miracle happened—one of the many miracles I have experienced in my life. My leg started healing.

During my stay in Brazil, I felt free. After all, being on crutches and having only one leg was a great conversation starter when meeting strangers and making new friends. I enjoyed the attention I got from my family and the people at the hotel. I even learned to dance Brazilian Lambada! I was happy to start a new chapter in my

life, but then reality hit me. I was terrified when I had to go to school on crutches without a prosthetic leg because the wound hadn't yet healed well enough. I didn't want people to see me and I certainly did not want to go to school. My older sister said that she would protect me, and that made me made me feel a little better. I agreed to go as long as my white school uniform was long enough to cover my stump.

Finally in April of 1987, I got my prosthetic leg. I was so excited! I felt like a child on Christmas day. After the painful process of learning how to walk, my stump lost weight drastically. I had to wear fifteen socks to make the prosthetic fit, which aggravated my skin condition. My leg would bleed constantly, not allowing me to enjoy any activity. I was devastated. For years, I had been told that I would be able to walk when I got a prosthetic leg, but I was still suffering tremendously. What if I would never be normal? What if I was destined to be in pain, and the only way to live was just to find acceptance? Many times, I wondered in desperation, "Why did this happen to me? What did I do to deserve this?" Over time, I learned to deal better with my situation, but I was miserable for a long time.

Most of my life, I lived in a prison within myself. I felt humiliated that people would see me struggle. Little by little, I started coming out of my cocoon. When I started to work out at the gym, I realized that the prison I was living in had a door—and it wasn't even locked! I had never tried to open it because of fear.

I grew up with only one leg in the poorest Latin American country—where one out of eight Bolivians lives on less than $1.25 of U.S. money per day and 59% of the population lives in extreme

poverty. How did I create the life of my dreams and own a multi-million dollar company next to my husband? What was the secret to my success?

1 **Have a vision.** When I was told the only way I would ever be somewhat normal would be to amputate my deformed leg, the only thing I could think of was the end result. While I was suffering in the hospital after my leg was amputated, I would visualize myself walking on my new prosthetic leg. I dreamed of the possibility of wearing a normal pair of shoes. I could feel myself walking on my two legs and being able to do things as simple as crossing my legs. Despite the pain I faced as a child—both emotionally and physically—I never stopped dreaming. One of my biggest visions was to leave Bolivia against everyone's wishes and create a better life for myself in the United States—and I did just that by visualizing it and following the steps I mention here.

2 **Achieve your goals one by one.** It's important to set goals and define sub-goals so you can achieve them one by one. It took me a while to convince my parents that the amputation was going to be the best solution for me. That was the first step to achieving one of my first major goals. Check yourself on a daily basis and do something productive to achieve the sub-goals you defined. There are only twenty-four hours in a day, so you have to use your time productively. Make a priority to dedicate at least one hour a day toward your sub-goals.

Ever since we met eight years ago, my husband and I have worked together through thick and thin by using each other's strengths and setting goals. When I was flying back and forth from Los Angeles to New York to get my prosthetic leg done, the owner brought up jokingly that my husband and I should start a new division to manufacture prosthetics since we already owned a company that worked with orthopedic doctors. It was just an idea—and idea that sounded impossible because there would be so much involved to make it reality— yet we made it happen. You must work hard for your dreams and surround yourself with people who believe in you and your vision.

 Overcome the obstacles you face. Focus on what you want and be determined. I was filled with disappointment and embarrassment when I had to go to school with one leg and crutches. Then when I finally got my prosthetic, it was tremendously painful. Many years later, I was able to get the prosthetic leg that I had envisioned my whole life but didn't even know existed. Because I refused to give up, I got the second silicone high heel leg created by a company in New York that was experimenting with silicon skins. Finally, I had a prosthetic that didn't hurt and looked so real that I was able to become a model without people noticing I was an amputee!

The goal-setting steps I used have led me to the wonderful life I live today. My husband and I have two amazing, healthy boys. We

own a prosthetic and orthotic company in Los Angeles, helping others like me to improve the quality of their lives.

I never stopped setting and working toward my goals, and even though my path hasn't been easy, it has made me the person I am today. It's helped me to grow and excel. I learned to hide the pain and channel it into achievements. With a lot of hard work, courage, and vision, I have found myself living the life I always dreamed – and you can too!

— ABOUT THE AUTHOR —

Elizabeth Bress-VonderHaar is the Vice President of Specialized Orthopedic Solutions, Inc. and has been responsible for developing the Prosthetic Division. Elizabeth represented Bolivia as Mrs. Bolivia International 2004 and had a successful career as an actress and model. The obstacles Elizabeth had to overcome in the pursuit of her dreams have fueled her desire to assist others. Elizabeth is the co-founder of www.sendingoutansos.org and is on the Board of Directors of www.ayuda.org, helping orphaned children in Latin America. She is a key supporter of Centro De Miembros Artificiales Bolivia, (http://www.rotaryboliviaprosthetics.org/sending_out_an_sos.html) helping Bolivian amputees to get back on their feet. www.sosmedical.net.

CHAPTER 21

Create Your Dream Life Using Three Quick Daily Habits

By Monique Kainth

"When your desires are strong enough, you will appear to possess superhuman powers to achieve." – Napoleon Hill

I was a gorgeous spring day. The sun was shining, and the birds were singing. As the balmy breeze caressed my face, a waft of the perfumed lilac bush nearby reminded me that my family was having a picnic in Duke Gardens. Yet here I was, sitting in my car waiting for my clients to finish taking measurements of their future home. Though my clients were wonderful people and I enjoyed my work, I didn't really want to spend yet another weekend away from my family. I wanted to go to the movies and brunch with them. I felt torn between my work and my family life, as I knew I was missing out on precious time that I could never get back.

I had worked hard to become a top producer within a short span of my real estate career. Switching careers was not appealing, because I didn't want to lose the client base and the reputation that I had built with such care and dedication. Suddenly, a quote from Napoleon Hill's book *Think and Grow Rich* popped into my head: "Whatever the mind can conceive and believe, it can achieve." At that moment, I decided to do something to create a better balance between my professional and personal life. I knew many people with a similar dilemma. I realized that once I found a way to overcome this challenge, I would be able to help others as well.

My first step was to come up with some creative ideas to deal with my challenge. To accomplish this, I developed certain tools. I created several guided meditations, along with other daily routines specific to my goals, and started practicing them diligently. It was important for me to keep these routines short for easy compliance.

Over a period of just a few weeks, I started getting insights, which I trusted and acted upon. I was inspired to take the necessary steps to get my real estate broker's license. Soon after I got my license, I started my own real estate company. Though this was not an easy process, I persevered by taking one step at a time. Gradually, I was able to hire realtors to work for me, thus freeing up my weekends and allowing me to spend more time with my family. It also enabled me to pursue other passions, such as traveling and coaching. As more and more people started to ask me about the secrets of my success, I decided to become a Transformational Success Coach and fulfilled my dream of training under Jack Canfield, co-author

of the *Chicken Soup for the Soul* books and America's top success coach. Now, I get to help people accomplish their most cherished goals, which is extremely gratifying for me.

> *"Only a life lived for others is a life worthwhile."*
> *– Albert Einstein*

Getting Started

Have you ever felt torn between your work and family life? Do you sometimes wish that there were two of you? If so, the following information might benefit you. Would you like to have more clarity and learn how to set your goals in a way that will bring them into reality faster?

It's important to set goals that are aligned with your life purpose. There are many ways you can discover your life purpose, but in my practice, the three most pertinent questions I ask my clients are:

1. What are some of the goals you have achieved in life that have given you a sense of accomplishment?
2. How can you help others achieve similar success?
3. How could you be of most service to others at this time in your life?
4. For me, the answers to these questions were clear. I was constantly being asked how I was able to achieve more personal time and create a better work/family balance. I knew that this was where I could be of most service to others at present. Life is an evolutionary process, so your life purpose could change

over time. Therefore, it's important to keep asking yourself the above questions on a regular basis. My goal of becoming a success coach aligned me with my life purpose, which in turn has given me the opportunity to live my dream life with more financial freedom than I ever imagined possible.

Three Simple Techniques with Profound Effects

After you have defined your life purpose and created goals that are aligned with it, the next step is to create daily habits that will support the fruition of those goals. Here are three of the techniques and a daily action plan to show you how to incorporate them into your life:

1 **Meditation – Develop your inner gps and take inspired actions.** Meditation is a great tool to develop your intuition. The answers you're seeking come to you more easily when you meditate on a regular basis.

Studies done by Yale, Harvard, and Massachusetts General Hospital reveal that the brain scans of those who meditate regularly have an increased thickness of gray matter in the parts of the brain that are responsible for attention and processing sensory input. This allows the brain to process more data, thereby developing intuition.

You will notice that as you start practicing meditation, creative thoughts will begin to occur spontaneously and more frequently. Become aware of this phenomenon and start taking actions based on these thoughts.

The meditation process doesn't have to be long or complicated; it can be just five minutes spent in silence with your attention directed inward. I have created several guided visualizations for quick results, which can be downloaded from my website: www.moniquekainth.com.

"The only real valuable thing is intuition." – Albert Einstein

Breathing techniques - Create focus and get rid of procrastination. There are several breathing techniques taken from yoga that I use in my practice to develop focus of the mind and to get rid of procrastination and inertia. One of my favorites is *Ujjayi,* or the Ocean Breath. The great thing about this breathing technique is that it can be practiced anywhere, even while walking or standing. It fills your body with life energy, and daily practice will bring vitality and focus into your life.

Sit or stand comfortably, keeping your mouth closed. Inhale slowly through both of your nostrils while partially closing your epiglottis. Properly done, it sounds like the ocean, thereby giving it the nickname "ocean breath." Fill the space between your throat and heart with this breath. Retain the breath as long as you comfortably can and then exhale through your nostrils, expanding your chest. It may take some practice before you become proficient with this breathing technique, but the results are well worth it.

"Breathing, according to me, corresponds to taking charge of one's own life." – Luce Irigaray

3 **Gratitude – Develop a positive mindset to attract abundance and prosperity**. The action of a thankful heart sets off a reaction of receiving. Thanking is appreciating. The more we appreciate what we receive, the more it appreciates (increases in value) for us. Deep and profound gratitude cannot be left unanswered. Albert Einstein is said to have had a practice of saying "thank you" hundreds of times a day. An attitude of gratitude will keep your mind positive.

"The grateful outreaching of your mind is a liberation or expenditure of force, it cannot fail to reach that to which it is addressed, and the reaction is an instantaneous movement towards you." – Wallace D. Wattles

The Daily Action Plan

The three techniques mentioned above will accelerate the manifestation of your goals, if you are consistent in practicing them on a daily basis.

✳ Meditate five minutes in the morning, as soon as you wake up, and five minutes just before you go to bed. You can just sit still and focus inward, or you can listen to a guided visualization.

* After meditating in the morning, do two sets of ten Ocean Breaths. Before meditating at night, do two more sets of ten Ocean Breaths.

* In the morning, when you are done with your breathing exercise, give thanks for five things you would like to achieve that day as if you've already achieved them. At night, after the breathing exercise and meditation, give thanks for five things that happened during the day or that you have in your life.

We often block our own receiving due to our internal blocks, and these techniques can help you discover and eliminate those blocks. In my case, after doing some inner work, I realized that I had several subconscious limiting beliefs that I acquired growing up that were causing sabotage in the achievement of my goals. For example, as a child, I had adopted a belief that I have to work really hard to make money. Once I changed that belief, my inner GPS was able to lead me on a fast track to success.

If you think that you might be blocking your own receiving due to subconscious fears and limiting beliefs, and would like to put your manifesting on a fast track, you can call me for a complimentary thirty-minute consultation. Through my customized process, you will be able to quickly:

* Dismantle the limiting beliefs that may be causing self-sabotage in your life.

* Discover your life purpose and (hidden) passions.

* Develop a powerful inner GPS system that will guide you to your dreams.

* Create goals that are aligned with your life purpose and a roadmap for achieving them.
* Create a customized daily routine incorporating individualized meditations, affirmations, and breathing techniques to open your heart to receiving the success you deserve.

— ABOUT THE AUTHOR —

Monique Kainth is a highly successful entrepreneur, a sought-after success coach, and an international leadership consultant. She travels throughout the world facilitating workshops, speaking, and coaching. Monique is passionate about creating breakthroughs in her clients' lives, thereby helping them achieve their most cherished goals. Her unique and proven coaching techniques can quickly demolish mental blocks to get rid of recurring patterns of self-sabotage. For a free thirty-minute consultation, please contact her at monique@ moniquekainth.com. If you would like to download a free assessment questionnaire and a short meditation MP3, please visit her website: www.moniquekainth.com.

CHAPTER 22

Step Forward and Overcome

By Brande Atkinson

> *"Nothing can dim the light which shines from within."*
> *- Maya Angelou*

Like many children in America, I grew up in a dysfunctional family. My mother was on welfare and did what she could to scrape by. However, I soon realized that she and my stepfather sold and used drugs. My family life was full of anger, physical and emotional abuse, and neglect. We lived in a trailer and exemplified the stereotype of "trailer trash." We are often conditioned to believe that someone from that background is broken, trashy, and worthless. But we are NOT our past!

My family showed me how to live a welfare mentality and to do illegal activities to get what they wanted out of life, yet I knew very early on that I wanted a better life. I knew that you could have happiness without using drugs or being a criminal. However,

as a teenager, I found myself veering down that very same path. I was in a lot of pain emotionally, and my job at Dairy Queen wasn't paying the bills. You so easily become a product of your environment if you allow it.

At that time, I was unaware that human trafficking existed. Nobody really talked about it twenty years ago, and I certainly had never expected that I would become a victim of it. Thankfully, when I was entrapped in this nightmare, I felt God pulling me out. I found the light and followed it, knowing I could create a better future. When you find yourself in a situation you don't think you can escape from, have faith that you can overcome any obstacle in your life.

In the past I had been encouraged to join the Air Force, but I was scared. After this life-changing event, I made the decision to alter the course of my life. I wanted be proud of myself instead of living on welfare and doing illegal things. After all, I had always detested how my family chose the "dark" side of life. There was a military base in my town and one day I finally got the courage to enlist and joined the military, leaving my boyfriend, my dog, my family, and my old life behind to embark on a new journey. The military motivated me to get involved in my community, further my education, and to develop myself professionally.

My journey has taught me valuable lessons: Regardless of your past or current circumstances, you can go for your dreams by setting goals. Even if you grew up with people who didn't have goals, or you had a lot of negativity around you, you can still achieve your dreams by really understanding yourself and being

clear on what you want in life. Many women who have been the victims of abuse of any kind hate themselves. Keep your vision in front of you and know that you can overcome negative feelings and build confidence by applying these valuable lessons:

* **Love yourself! Believe in yourself!** Many people don't move toward their dream because they don't allow themselves success and joy. If you think you don't deserve it, you'll sabotage yourself, and you'll never achieve your goals. You have to love yourself enough that you know you deserve what is in your heart. You are unique, and you have unique talents and abilities. Somebody needs you.

* **We're able to give what we feel inside.** If you don't think you're loved, especially by God, it's hard to share that love. Know that you are worthy and special. There may be other people doing the same thing, but people will be attracted to who you are. You deserve to be and have what you want because you have this loving heart.

* **Change your thoughts.** It can be a challenge for people to open their mind and believe. Get your eyes off yourself and focus on how you can impact others. Stop comparing yourself, thinking that others are better than you. Tell yourself, "If she can do it, I can do it." Get yourself out of the way, and don't make it about you. Success means making a difference in somebody else's life. Just making money isn't success. Making an impact is what really matters.

* **Give yourself permission to be new.** Perfectionism will kill creation. If you expect to be perfect when you're new, you won't move forward. It's okay to be new at the beginning. Don't be hard on yourself, as you need time to grow. Tell yourself, "I'm growing. I'm ahead of where I was last week or last month." You can't compare yourself with somebody who may have been doing something for ten years when you are just starting out. Sometimes you don't feel like creating because your first thing may not be your best work, and you're scared of what other people may think. Perfectionism creeps in and causes self-doubt. You have to overcome black and whiteness. It won't be perfect the first time, and that is ok. You'll tweak it, and it will improve.

* **Surround yourself with like-minded people.** Make friends with people who are on the same journey—who believe in you and in what you are creating. When you see others having success, it reignites your passion and inspires you. It helps you to keep going—to keep believing—because you see the end result of what is possible for you too. If you are struggling with self-doubt, procrastination, or lack of belief, remind yourself, "If he can do it, I can too." Finding a mentor to guide you on your path is very valuable because you can avoid pitfalls and achieve your goals faster.

When I see my old high school friends who are still doing what they were doing twenty years ago, I'm so grateful that I joined the Air Force. Being around people who set a higher

standard for themselves and were committed to growth helped me to become a better person: I've built self-esteem and changed my behavior.

❋ **Have a plan and take action.** Your plan doesn't have to be perfect. Even if you don't know exactly how to write a plan, do it anyway. Research what is needed, map it out, and continue to take action toward your goal. Being really clear about what you want and writing it out will also help. You need to know the steps it takes to get where you want to go. It's easy to get side-tracked; just keep the next step in front of you so you won't get distracted along the way. Look at the next step.

Success requires tenacity. Most of it is in your mind, and you have to keep going whether you feel like it or not. When you stumble, get up and keep going again. The word discipline means more than doing a routine. It means you do what you have to, even when you don't feel like it. You have to be willing to do what it takes.

When your goals are in alignment with your passion, you'll be living an authentic life. My life is an example that you don't have to be defined by your past, and you can love yourself to greatness. My hope is to inspire others to believe that they can have the life they desire, and it starts with self-love. We can't wipe away our past, but we can redefine who we are. We have the choice to be happy, make the necessary steps, and achieve our goals.

— ABOUT THE AUTHOR —

Brande Atkinson is a retired Air Force veteran, passionate entrepreneur, speaker, author, and coach. She earned her B.A. in psychology, and her military career cultivated her skills in leadership and development. She is a servant leader whose passion is helping others, whether in life or business. With over twenty years of sales and business experience, she helps to guide people to take their message to the world leveraging the Internet. She enjoys being a transformational coach and empowering people to create a life they love. She can be reached at www.brandeatkinson.com or brandeatkinson@gmail.com.

CHAPTER 23

The Sovereign Life

By Amy Masreliez

> *"The two most important days in your life are the day you were born and the day you find out why." – Mark Twain*

A young woman approached her father and said, "My father, you have been such a wonderful role model to me. You have taught me so much and helped me in so many ways. You have helped me develop healthy self-esteem, and I feel I can go out and conquer the world. I can compete, play in sports, and do anything a man can do. Thank you, father."

Her father returned her glance and said, "My dear, come sit close. I believe that you have the capacity to fulfill all of your dreams, but there is one more thing you must know."

"Yes, father?" She replied.

He said, "Your life is filled with mirrors, reflecting back to you illusions and stories of the past. Don't get caught up in them. By

being present in the moment, you'll find your inner purpose. As you walk down this hall of mirrors, one day you will reach a door, and you will not know how to open it. I have given you all of the tools and resources necessary to understand how to navigate through life. When that door comes, darling, you will have the desire to crawl under it, go through it and climb over it, with everything that I have taught you. There is one secret you need to know to open the door—there is a key. This key, my daughter, is your heart. The key to all of your relationships—the wisdom of unlocking your true potential in your life—is found in your heart. Go out, my dear, and conquer the world. But always remember that the highest calling is in your heart."

After extensive research and experience as an entrepreneur, I have reached the same conclusion as the father in the story above: Your greatest potential and fulfillment is realized when you connect with your inner purpose, the essence of your deepest self. Your inner purpose is best aligned with the outer purpose, to fulfill a life vision of Purpose, Presence and Prosperity – to live the Sovereign Life. Living a Sovereign Life means choosing a path that is not based on old conditioning or expectations. You will own your life and not be trapped into doing what your parents did or what society expects you to do. Success and being of value to others in the world does not exist as a specific goal outcome; rather, it is a quality of Being.

Designing a Destiny

When I was twelve years old, I was riding my bike home from school one day, and I was hit by a car. Though I suffered a three-inch fracture of my skull, I healed and regenerated remarkably quickly. After my accident, I changed. Was it the accident? I don't honestly know. My parents noticed that I became more driven, focused, and goal-oriented following the accident. I started caring less about impressing others or what high society thought of me coming from a middle-class household. While my friends made regular excursions to their ski chalets and tropical destinations, I immersed myself in self-awareness. While they were taking academic excursions to Washington D.C., I was gathering clues from my deepest essence of Being.

In order to unleash your full potential and accomplish your dreams and goals, you must uncage your mind and follow your heart's desire. That's what I did. By the age of seventeen, I had become a self-pronounced vegan. I was adept in self-hypnosis, practicing meditation and Tai Chi before school. It was in 1989, the same year that the Berlin Wall came down, that I first looked within to tear down the walls of my own past and design a life. I was inspired to take a train to Seattle with $100 in my pocket and a plan to architect my future.

When I left home, I wasn't running from the past. I was following my intuition without compromise, along with the parental encouragement of my self-determination. From there, I self-funded my future, became a global change leader at

Microsoft Corporation, and started two successful consulting businesses, all while marrying and learning to raise a beautiful, loving family.

I learned that true success is a way of Being, involving the understanding of inner purpose aligned to balanced goals in all areas of life. You may be wondering, "How does relocating give insight into one's life purpose?" Of course, once you experience your core truth, you are able to make your own magic wherever you are. For me, I was able to let go of old stories and observe the present moment with crystal clarity. "Can I let go of stories defining my identity without changing?" Sometimes, listening and taking action without compromise of being requires getting outside your comfort zone. The physical move was a growth catalyst, and the far greater impact was my attunement to the intelligence of the heart.

"The heart has reasons that reason does not understand."
– Jacques Benigne Bossuet

Knowing Yourself and Your Heart's Desire

Are your goals truly aligned to your heart's desire? If you listen to your heart, you can determine your inner purpose in life. Once you know this and connect it to your outer purpose, you will become endowed with spiritual power. You will no longer have to find a way to go over, around, under, or through any obstacle that gets in your way. You will no longer have to wonder whether anything can stop you from achieving your goals. This is

because your goal attainment will not be based upon willpower, determination, or struggle. It will become effortless as the field of Being at one with the totality orchestrates your newfound reality into existence. This is the feminine way of manifestation, where your energy field connects with the collective energy field. You will attract what you have become.

In every society, happiness is often measured through a target, such as a role, title, relationship, or status symbol. We are so conditioned to this idea of doing that we tend to ignore our inner voices of Being. When our goals do not align with our inner purpose, we rob ourselves and the world of our true impact and the fulfillment that comes with leaving a remarkable legacy.

Real and lasting success comes from within. A burning desire and persistence originate naturally and effortlessly from the soul passion that is connected to a deeper purpose. The key is listening to and trusting intuition, with which everyone is blessed when they are born. Don't let anything get in the way of hearing your inner voice and reaching your true potential.

For me, the hidden key was learning to allow myself to be open and vulnerable, rather than just tough and bulletproof. I had built an identity around being industrious, self-reliant, responsible, and independent, which masked my inner diamond. I had to believe that my potential would unfold naturally with faith.

Tap into your true potential and find what is keeping you from sharing your life and gifts with those around you. You don't have to travel to Tibet on a monastic journey, go to an ashram in India,

or become a yoga instructor in order to silence your mind, connect to Presence, find your true essence, and change what is preventing you from living your dreams. I am not saying you shouldn't do those things, but don't think that they are necessary for evolution or that they are the golden ticket to enlightenment. By being mindful of yourself and attuning to the Present, your inner voice of the Spirit offers direction. Trust your intuition to find your talents, latent capabilities, and true north. Then align your beliefs with your inner and outer life purpose. This congruence will allow you to seize and respond to life's challenges and opportunities. Embracing the unknown, living a life of adventure, and choosing to play with your goals in life are all possible. Live a life by design, rather than a life by default.

"Until you make the unconscious conscious, it will direct your life and you will call it fate." — Carl Jung

The Vibrational Frequency of your Emotions

The vibrational frequency of our field of Being is connected to our emotions, and is often rooted or masked in our unconscious. This frequency impacts our ability to visualize consistently and create our dreams. Lower vibrational frequencies, which come from negative core emotions like fear, lead the world into separation and chaos. Higher frequencies, with one of the highest coming from love, lead to joy and peace. In his book *Power vs. Force*, David R. Hawkins explains that people often emit nearly

the same frequencies their entire life, and the majority of the world has a low vibrational frequency. However, according to Hawkins, we have the possibility of increasing that frequency immensely, in any area of our lives, by becoming conscious of our emotions and purifying or releasing the energy of them from our field. The more our plans are attuned to the evolutionary creative force and unity of life, the greater the possibility of goal attainment.

Are You Coming From the Heart?

The feminine side of leadership—leading from the heart—is in demand now more than ever. Women and men are beginning to embrace their feminine side in business *and* in life. The Pulitzer Prize winning journalist Michael D'Antonio and best-selling co-author John Gerzema[1] discovered that the skills people think we need to thrive in today's world are widely regarded as more feminine skills. The authors surveyed populations that represent 65% of the world's domestic product. The authors intentionally sought a wide range of cultural, geographical, political, religious, and economic perspectives. The values and skills people believed were most valuable in business included honesty, empathy, communication, appreciation, and collaboration. All of these attributes are widely regarded as being on the feminine side of human nature, both historically—as recognized by cultural anthropologists—and in contemporary times, as recognized by modern neuroscientists.

---

1 1 D'Antonio Michael and Gerzema, John. (2013) Athena Doctrine: How Women, And The Men Who Think Like Them, Will Rule The Future.

The authors assert that the hyper-masculine era in leadership is coming to an end. In a sense, the world is achieving balance.

Studies show that employees in the United States are rarely engaged in the goals of the company they work for. They don't care about the companies they work for, and their employers are not reaching their hearts. By integrating masculine and feminine energies, you can improve your work life, because it sets the course for profoundly impactful and powerful goals that come from the heart. Integrating the heart in leadership brings great benefits.

"I think we need the feminine qualities of leadership, which include attention to aesthetics and the environment, nurturing, affection, intuition, and the qualities that make others feel safe and cared for." – Deepak Chopra

Where Do We Go From Here?

We live in a time of great opportunity to expand awareness into new paradigms of growth, as well as find greater possibilities to contribute to the world. We just need to quiet the mind, connect to our hearts, and live a life from our core essence. To do this, simply ask your heart a question to set a clear intention: "How can I be of the greatest service to humanity?" Then you must live the answer. Since we cannot see the details of the journey ahead, we have to trust in the direction that our intention takes, even if it does not make sense to us at the time. This is the path to leading a life of Purpose, Presence and Prosperity – The Sovereign Life.

When this happens, the impact we can make is vast. We can inspire others to action, establish authority from authenticity, and liberate our own joyful creativity. Ultimately, through service, we can still the wave of collective emotional chaos and retrain our brains to activate a higher consciousness of humanity. As Abraham Lincoln said, "In order to lead a man to your cause, you must first reach his heart, the great high road to reason." Leading others becomes an effortless proposition when you are aligned with the heart. The stored-up energy and potential within a single human being is infinite in its proportions. By accessing stillness of the mind and leading your life from the heart, you may eventually find yourself in a position to experience oneness with all of Creation. This is the eternal now, the unity of stillness and bliss from which all visions become manifest. Access your key to the Sovereign Life.

— ABOUT THE AUTHOR —

Amy Masreliez is a social entrepreneur, speaker, wellness expert, and success coach. She is the founder of OM Lifestyle and creator of The Sovereign Life. She serves as a consultant and advisor to purpose-driven entrepreneurs and life and health coaches. For more than twenty years, Amy has offered expert guidance on IT, strategy, and leadership for clients like Microsoft and the Federal Reserve. Learn more about her forthcoming book and podcast series, The Sovereign Life, at: http://www.amymasreliez.com.

CHAPTER 24

Imagine and Succeed

By John Assaraf

"Imagination is the beginning of creation. You imagine what you desire, You will what you imagine, and at last you create what you will." – George Bernard Shaw

Imagine yourself at a beautiful beach—palm trees, white sand, and the gentle roar of the waves slapping against the shoreline. Or perhaps you watch the Travel Channel, and you see yourself scuba diving in Belize with schools of bright, cheerfully-colored fish swarming around you. Using the power of your imagination by visualizing on a daily basis, you can create the life you truly want by setting clear, precise goals and then consciously focusing your thoughts, feelings, and taking positive actions on them daily.

To start, you need to have an absolutely clear vision of exactly what it is you want to create. You can design it in any way you want. Exercise your imagination, creativity, and ingenuity—have

fun with it! There is no limitation to your imagination. As you create a clear vision of your future, you will begin to see things you have never seen before. Miracles will happen! The key is to program your mind with visualizations, emotions, and specific affirmations that support the new vision and goals you have. By regularly repeating empowering new beliefs, they will be engraved deep in your subconscious mind.

The ideal state for achieving your goals is to be motivated from deep within—to wake up excited every day—to enjoy the adventure you will have on the way to success. To motivate yourself to take action, consider how achieving your goals will make you feel. How will you act, walk, and talk when you have achieved each goal? What will you do with your new life? Come up with as many positive reasons and anchors as possible to motivate you to do your best. Don't just sit on the sidelines waiting for things to change; take charge and make your dreams come true.

Creating a vision board, which is basically a board with cut-out pictures that accurately depict the various goals you want to reach can solidify in your mind the mental image of what you want to achieve and helps you focus on how to achieve it. There are many reasons that vision boards are so effective. Here are three of them:

1. The more specific and clear your goal is in your mind, the easier it is to achieve it.

2. If you see your goal in front of you on a regular basis, you will be more motivated to act on it.

3. When you are motivated to reach a clear, specific goal, it's easier to commit to it.

The vision board is a reminder of the power that comes from setting goals. As a matter of fact, writing down your goals is the first step toward achieving them. Why is this? When you write down your goals, your mind begins to focus on what you want—and perhaps more importantly, what you *don't* want starts to recede into the past. The more specific you are when deciding your goals, the more clearly your mind can grasp what you're after. When that happens, it will get easier for you to differentiate between things that will help you reach your goals and things that will distract you from them.

Take a moment to ask yourself, *"What do I want to achieve in a year? Five years? Ten? Twenty?"* Write down your goals and make a timeline for when you want to achieve each one. Then start to make a plan. What can you do today, tomorrow, this week, next week, and so on that will move you closer to reaching those goals? It will take time and planning to figure out what it is that you really want to do, but it is definitely worth it. Remember the old expression, "Poor planning leads to poor performance." When you focus your mind on your goals every day, and you have a plan of action for accomplishing them, you will find yourself moving toward your goals and eliminating the unnecessary things that are holding you back from reaching them.

Design your vision and write out your goals until they are perfect on paper and in your mind, then create your vision board. Plan for success, and then take action. Every time you set your

goals higher, stay focused and make sure you're imprinting them on your subconscious mind. Allow them to work for you!

What if you still find yourself procrastinating or not reaching your goals? George Naope, a great kahuna of Hawaii, says, "Take responsibility for everything that happens in your life, everything good and everything bad, as if you created it." This can be a tough concept to swallow, but the benefits are undeniable. When you take responsibility in this manner, every event in your life becomes an opportunity for feedback and improvement on the deepest of levels. Why are you dragging your feet? What excuses have you made for yourself? Pay attention to how you feel when you voice aloud what your goals are. Do they pump you up? Sometimes it can be that we are pursuing goals that we are not really in alignment with. If it turns out that they're not really something that you want deep inside, change directions and go for something that you *do* want.

Once you know that your goals are ones that you really want, stay focused and commit to doing the neural reconditioning work day in and day out. Make yourself reminder notes to review where you stand with the process, perhaps at the beginning of every week. Add a statement to your reprogramming routine that addresses your commitment—something along the lines of "I am building on a solid, new, unconscious foundation to take my success even further."

So, in review: Write down your goals and come up with a plan to achieve them. Focus on your goals constantly. Create your own vision board to reinforce your goals on a subconscious level. If you find yourself suffering from a lack of motivation, examine

your goals to make sure they're really what you want—if they're not, find new ones! Keep yourself flexible and open to any possible means of achieving your goals, not just what you think you need to do. And finally, after you have achieved what you wanted, set new, higher goals for yourself and start the process over again. If you do this, you will see the benefits of visualization in your own life, and you will reach your goals. Don't ever ask yourself if you are worthy of your goals, ask if your goals are worthy of you, and then act boldly to achieve those goals.

— ABOUT THE AUTHOR —

John Assaraf, a leader in the area of spiritual entrepreneurship, has built five multi-million-dollar businesses in the last twenty years. John's passions are his family, spirituality, exercise, cooking, travel, and helping entrepreneurs understand how to incorporate the psychological and strategic sides of building a successful business and life into their plans. You can learn more about John and his groundbreaking brain research and approach to earning more money and living your ideal life at www.praxisnow.com.

Write, Inspire, Prosper –
Become an Author!

*N*o doubt you have been inspired and empowered by the incredible stories from the authors of this book. Not only do they show that everything is possible, they give the step-by-step process to succeed in your own life!

Would you like to inspire others with your story?
Do you have a message to share?
What knowledge do you have that others can benefit from?

Maybe you have been thinking about writing a book, maybe it has been one of your dreams for many years, but you didn't know where to start. We are here to help!

It is our mission to help thought-leaders capture their messages on paper and inspire the world.

Whether you want to write your own book or become a coauthor, you will benefit greatly from being an author, especially when you are a business owner.

Contact us today! Send an email to
Shamayah@CoAuthorswanted.com.
Www.coauthorswanted.com

* **Touch lives** – You can reach people who may have never heard about you if you had not written your story in a book.
* **Get instant credibility** – Authors are respected in our society. You will be known as the author-ity in your industry.
* **Become the expert** – Stand out from the competition and attract more clients.
* **Grow your business** – People want to do business with someone they like and trust. Your book can generate leads and will help to build rapport with new prospects.
* **Get free publicity** – Authors are often invited on radio and TV shows to share their expertise.
* **Receive recognition** – Friends, family, clients and business relations will perceive you differently when you are an author. You'll gain more respect.
* **Leave your legacy** – Your words and life lessons will be preserved for generations to come just like Napoleon Hill's powerful words are still being read by millions of people.

Did you enjoy reading this book?

Make sure you download your FREE GIFT that can change your life at www.HappinessisaVerb.com/SIYV2.0

Please do us a huge favor and post a great review on Amazon.

If you would like to read more inspirational stories, buy also:

Step into Your Vision
Top Business Leaders Share their Goal Setting Secrets

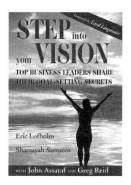

The Diamond from Within
Overcoming Obstacles in Life and Business

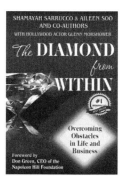